A Tale of Two Ports

Dedication

This book is dedicated to all who work in the port transport industry, managers and workpeople alike, and particularly to those many in the ports of London and Southampton with whom I have been privileged to work and to call my friends.

A Tale of Two Ports

London
and
Southampton

John Hovey

With a foreword by Sir Ronald Swayne, MC

The Industrial Society

First published 1990 by
The Industrial Society
Robert Hyde House
48 Bryanston Square
London W1H 7LN
Telephone 071-262-2401

British Library Cataloguing in Publication Data
Hovey, John
   A tale of two ports.
   1. London. Ports : Port of London, history   2. Hampshire.
   Southampton. Ports : Port of Southampton, history
   I. Title
   387.109421

   ISBN 0-85290-908X

Typeset by Action Typesetting Ltd, Gloucester
Jacket designed by Chambers Chapman Design Associates and printed by Belmont Press Ltd, Northampton
Printed and bound in Great Britain by Alden Press Ltd, Oxford

Contents

Foreword

by Sir Ronald Swayne, MC

Britain needs trade, and trade needs the smooth and rapid handling of goods through our ports. The latter was a circumstance on which, for 40 years after World War II, industry and commerce were unable to rely, except in those ports which escaped public ownership and the National Dock Labour Scheme. Our exporters were at a much greater disadvantage in this respect than their competitors overseas.

It would be wrong to lay the blame wholly on either the employers or the dockers, or even on both of them. The roots of the problem were political and social: they included the Great Hunger in Ireland, slums in port areas, the rapid expansion of maritime trade in much larger ships, the use of great numbers of Irish labourers – most of whom remained after their work was done – to dig the new docks, and the daily hiring of manpower out of a pool of unskilled men which always exceeded demand because the ports were the last resort of the unemployed. The roots lay too deep for an easy solution. They were nurtured by bad legislation and ill conceived intervention in disputes by governments of both major political parties, worried about the effect prolonged stoppages would have on the pound.

In the period covered, the dockers were far from all bloody-minded (although they represented fertile soil for trouble-makers) and their leaders were often men of great ability like Ernest Bevin, Frank Cousins and Jack Jones. Although with some employers old attitudes died hard, employers' leaders like Lord Sanderson and Sir Andrew Crichton sought peace and efficiency and had an understanding of the dockers' views and sympathised with them.

The mechanisation of port handling, when we set in hand the container revolution, offered both the risk of even more damaging confrontation and the possibility at last of a new and sensible modern relationship between management and labour. No one understood this more vividly than John Hovey, with his experience and his belief in good industrial relations based on mutual understanding. He took on a position of great operational responsibility for creating and running what could prove to be the most successful container terminal in Europe, due to its site and to the double tides. The tragedy was that he was not given the key to complete success: the responsibility for creating a body of skilled men, permanently and directly employed by him, who could enjoy the same security and involvement in the enterprise as the rest of the people who worked for us. The influence of the National Dock Labour Scheme and the relationship between port authorities, terminal companies and shipowners prevented this.

John cheerfully tolerated all the difficulties, but he never lost sight of his objective: a harmonious relationship with the dockers working *for* him but not employed *by* him. Under the conditions which have now emerged he would have achieved this aim. It is a pity that he had to retire before the recent changes came about.

Despite their frequent exasperation with recurring troubles – which I much regret having myself expressed unfairly sometimes – the ship-owners never lost their respect for him or their confidence that he was doing all that could be done to resolve the problems. Nor was my great liking for John ever shaken. Industrial disruption in the port and some overmanning apart, the Southampton operation based on Solent Container Services was a success.

This is an authoritative account of an important page of British post-war economic history, written with the same authority, objectivity and honesty that John has always brought to his work.

Author's note

Since my manuscript has been completed the ports of both London and Southampton have faced a national dock strike, called by the TGWU as a result of the government's abolition of the National Dock Labour Scheme. The dockers sought a country-wide agreement with the employers to replace the scheme, whereas the employers insisted on differing local agreements to suit the conditions in the various ports.

I well remember advising my colleagues when I retired that the only remaining cause for major dissension in the docks would be the abolition of the scheme. Established after World War II for the best of motives, as a necessary antidote and corrective for the iniquities of the casual system, it had, with the decasualisation of the industry in 1967, outlived its usefulness, and should have been abolished there and then. That it was allowed to continue is ample evidence of the importance attached to it by both sides of the industry, but particularly by the dockworkers and their unions, who regarded it with good reason as sacrosanct, representing as it did all their struggles to free themselves from the exploitation they had suffered in the past.

In the years that followed decasualisation, the employers from time to time suggested amendments to the scheme to make it more acceptable in a modern technological age. They were unsuccessful. The dockers relied, not unnaturally, on the privileges which parliament had accorded them, and made it clear that to attack their 'sacred cow' would be to court disaster – in the shape of a national dock strike. Successive governments preferred to take the easy option of letting the scheme wither on the vine rather than face this challenge, and it therefore came as a surprise when ministers decided, in the spring of 1989, to press ahead with abolition.

I describe the effects of the scheme in some detail in the early parts of the book. It would be presumptuous of me to pass judgement on it. The one thing that can be said with confidence is that eventually the scheme had to go. One may deplore the method of its passing, but there is no doubt that it had become a serious impediment to the economic progress – perhaps even the survival – of the ports where the scheme operated. The reasons are twofold. First, it was by any standards grossly unfair that, through accident of history, the older ports should be shackled by the restrictions and expenses inherent in the scheme while other new ports, most notably Felixstowe, were able to profit by remaining outside it. A second important effect of the scheme was that, in the days of sophisticated and highly integrated terminal operations, it accorded to dockers a higher status than that of other equally important terminal workers, and thus prevented that complete and unquestioned interdependence between all the individuals in a team which is so vital to the team's success. In short, all ports had to be either in the scheme or out of it, and all employees in a port – many would include the managers in this – had to enjoy the same basic privileges and protection under the law. Dockers had rightly been awarded special protection against the rampant casualism of the past, but now that the past is over the ports must look instead to the future.

It is interesting that ports like London (Tilbury) and Southampton, each of which contain large, independently operated and potentially successful container terminals, which have little to lose and a great deal to gain by the abolition of the scheme, were in the van of opposition to the strike. Freed from those shackles that have bound them up until now, the container ports of London and Southampton should at last be able to face the future with confidence and, together with their great rival Felixstowe, provide a solid and reliable basis for the nation's container trade.

With the abolition of the scheme, one of the last links with conventional dock work has been broken. It is understandable that many dock workers should regret its passing, but the industry as a whole should now forget the past and seize with both hands the new freedom it has been given to compete and to prosper.

John Hovey
Lymington, July 1990

x

Acknowledgements

I am deeply indebted to Sir Ronald Swayne for writing a foreword to my book, and to the following people who have taken much time and trouble to read the proofs and to suggest amendments: Colonel P.A. Tobin, of OCL, John Williams and Malcolm Purgavie of ABP, Ernie Allen of the TGWU, Dick Butler and John Gabony of the Port of London Authority, and Dr Edwin Course of the University of Southampton.

I am indebted also to the Port of London Authority, the Museum in Docklands Project, Associated British Ports PLC and Southampton City Museums, as well as to P & O Containers Ltd, Ben Line (Containers) Ltd and Southampton Container Terminals Ltd, for allowing me to use photographs from their archives.

Lastly, I owe a very big thank you to my son Peter for doing my secretarial work, and above all to my wife Mattie for enduring long hours of silence when I was in the throes of writing this book.

Introduction

The recollections in this book have as their backcloth the ports of London and Southampton. The two ports share many things in common. Both were established in Roman times for strategic and trading reasons at key points – the one to command a crossing of the Thames, the other to take advantage of the confluence of the Test and the Itchen, allowing access by water through the thickly forested lowlands of the south to the settlements on the chalk uplands of Wessex. Both ports declined into obscurity during the Dark Ages and reemerged in medieval times as increasingly important places in terms of the defence of the realm and the conduct of trade, the one with the countries bordering the North Sea and the other with the opposite side of the English Channel.

As the centuries passed, and as the merchant adventurers based in the City of London spread their tentacles throughout the increasingly known world, the Port of London – with its massive domestic market close at hand and naturally at the hub of communications throughout the nation – rapidly outstripped the Solent port as a commercial centre. By the time of the Napoleonic Wars, the importance of the Solent area as a bulwark of the country's defence by sea had dwarfed its development as a trading port.

The coming of the Industrial Revolution accentuated these trends. In London the expanding requirements of trade necessitated the construction, from the 1790s onwards, of vast areas of impounded water for the handling of vessels of ever-increasing size. The 'enclosed docks' – as they came to be known – eventually stretched all the way from Tower Bridge to Tilbury and became, in a very real sense, the hub of the British Empire. These docks were all private speculative ventures, as was the custom of the day, and after the 1840s were largely built by Irish labour imported in the aftermath of the great potato famine, presumably because it was the cheapest labour available. Having built the docks these Irish men, in their thousands, looked to earn whatever they could by going to work in the docks they had constructed and by offering their labour on a day-to-day basis to load and unload the ships.

1

Southampton, isolated as it was from the main centres of population, continued to lag behind London, in the east, and Liverpool and Bristol, with their concentration on the trans-Atlantic trade, in the west. It was not until the coming of the railways that this geographical disadvantage was overcome. Then some ship-owners, particularly those in the passenger trades, saw advantage in escaping from the increasingly congested Port of London: there was also the added advantage that the narrow waters of the Straits of Dover and the long haul up the Thames estuary could be avoided – a factor of major importance in the days of sail and the early days of steam.

The expansion of Southampton began in the 1840s with the construction of docks for the safe mooring and handling of vessels, although these did not require to be enclosed, as in London, owing to the much greater depth of water available and to the unique natural feature of a 'double high tide'. From the outset the particular advantages of Southampton were deeper water, making the accommodation of larger vessels easier, and direct access to the English Channel and thence to the Atlantic. Both of these benefits made Southampton a natural port of call for the increasing numbers of passenger liners by now plying the oceans of the world, particularly those on the trans-Atlantic run. For nigh on 50 years at the end of the nineteenth century and into the twentieth century, as London continued to increase in size and importance as a commercial cargo port, Southampton supplanted Liverpool to become the premier passenger port of the kingdom.

In the two world wars both ports played strategic roles, London as the indispensable hub of trade and Southampton as a staging point, in World War I for supply of the Western Front and in World War II as a base for the Normandy invasion. In the latter war, particularly, both ports suffered grievous damage to both property and personnel.

It has been my privilege, during my working life, to come to know and love these ports. They have both had a famous history, more than their fair share of trials and tribulation, and little by way of understanding of their problems by the country at large. Having had 25 years' experience of the London scene followed by 15 years at Southampton, I hope to be able to set the record straight and, in so doing, to pay tribute to my many friends and acquaintances from both sides of the port transport industry.

LONDON

1 The pre-war days

Memory is a fickle jade, and yet it is the most potent weapon we have to help us convey personal impressions of the past. My earliest memories are those of contrast – contrast between the pleasant semi-rural Kentish suburbs where I was brought up and the grimy, often squalid, streets of dockland with their seemingly endless rows of smoke-blackened terraced housing, interspersed with towering factories and foundries, such windows as they had barred and forbidding, and their chimneys belching out clouds of acrid smoke by night and day. I can still recall the increasing murk and gloom, except on the brightest of days, as one approached the southern end of the Rotherhithe or Blackwall tunnel, and on many winter days – indeed sometimes for weeks on end – the gloom and the smoke would fuse into the almost total obscurity of a London 'pea-souper'.

I can remember, in the years immediately preceding World War II when the level of work and employment in the Port of London was near its peak, being driven by my father through the Rotherhithe Tunnel. It was an eerie experience. The roads in dockland were virtually all stone-paved with small setts over which the traffic bumped and groaned. Many of the smaller commercial vehicles were still horse-drawn, as were the lumbering brewers' drays. It was a regular occurence to crawl through the tunnel behind a dray or to meet one at a sharp corner in the middle of the tunnel, where the great wheels had to come well over the centre line of the road in order to negotiate the angle while the oncoming traffic waited. It was an unforgettable sight to see the great dray horses with the breath flaring from their nostrils, straining and heaving at the heavy vehicles, with the drayman, whip in hand, high against the roof of the tunnel. The metalled hooves clanged against the stone setts; the noise of the fans which sucked the fumes through large circular air-vents at the corners of the tunnel added to the hellish din and made conversation impossible.

The northern exit to the tunnel abutted onto Commercial Road, the main artery of traffic from all the docks of London to the City, the West

End and the vast market-place which lay beyond. All day and much of the night, it was an overflowing stream of commercial traffic of every kind, both motorised and horse-drawn. Lorries of every possible shape and size, and conveying every possible kind of merchandise, passed down this highway from Whitechapel to the West India Dock Road. From here the stream began to branch and disperse its burden to the many docks and onwards to destinations throughout the world.

Emerging from the tunnel we had to turn right into Commercial Road and join this flood of traffic. Commercial Road itself consisted mainly of terraced housing, becoming more decrepit and grimy as one proceeded eastward, moving from the business premises that seemed largely to be owned by Jewish tailors to those of the ship's chandlers and others who catered for the needs of ships and seamen. There were seamen's taverns, doss-houses and, like a shining beacon, the headquarters of the Flying Angel Mission in the Commercial Road.

We had to turn right again, into the West India Dock Road. This was as far as the trams went; here they debouched their teeming loads of dockers twice daily at the dock gates after a screeching journey over a steel track which other traffic had somehow to circumnavigate. Only the railway bridge carrying the Fenchurch Street to Blackwall line separated the tram-stop from the massive gates of the West India Dock. These were next to the official office of the superintendent of the dock. Although this building, surprisingly, had started life as a pub, it would not have shamed a colonial governor in its magnificence of design. It stood a few feet back from the street, protected by massive iron railings and gazing a little disdainfully on *The Blue Posts* opposite it and *Charlie Brown's* to its left. These were both traditional dockers' pubs, and in them many a deal was struck, a day's work found, a score settled or a bribe taken. Pennyfields, the Chinatown of London, where policemen walked in pairs and only the foolhardy ventured alone, was only a stone's throw away.

It was opposite *Charlie Brown's* and *The Blue Posts,* on the 'Stones', that the twice-daily 'call' for employment at the West India Docks took place. Many accounts of this practice have been given, and it is easy to recall a sea of faces, topped by flat caps – mostly black or grey – and wrapped in scarves or 'chokers', surging forward, union cards in hand, hoping to have them taken by one of a series of foremen representing various employers who sought to engage labour for a newly arrived ship. Those who found favour were guaranteed one day's work or more. Those who failed were turned away penniless: the welfare state had yet to be conceived. It is not difficult to imagine the degree of corruption, bribery and degradation which such a system engendered. It has all left an indelible impression on my mind.

My father's office was on the Pier Head at Millwall Dock. The situation was rather like working over the shop. To gain access to the dock from Limehouse Reach, any ship had to pass the office, and the captain could be greeted by my father or one of the family as he entered into our 'domain'.

To get to Pier Head from *Charlie Brown's* you had to turn right yet again, going beneath the railway bridge of the Fenchurch Street line and then entering a veritable canyon which extended all the way to Millwall. On the left towered the 20-foot-high wall surrounding the West India Dock, a wall built as a perpetual monument to the West India Dock Company and, I must assume, with the aim of keeping valuable goods in and unwelcome visitors out. The wall was to play an important part in the future history of dockland, as it contributed to the mystique surrounding dock work – a mystique that prevails to this day. On the right, equally high walls were broken only by intersecting canyons which gave access to a succession of wharves abutting onto the Thames; occasionally, through a network of cranes and dockside paraphernalia, one could catch a glimpse of the river.

It was through these deep and ill-lit canyons that the dockers' wages, paid daily (and, before World War I, in gold), had to be transported by my father from the bank in West Ferry Road to his office at Pier Head, there to be distributed among a seemingly endless line of stooped and cloth-capped figures through an aperture just large enough for the clerk's glance of recognition and for an outstretched palm. The conveyance itself was a hazardous task because of the risk of robbery, and on winter evenings, when the fog obscured the alleyways off the West Ferry Road, my father was invariably accompanied by the local constable.

My father's stevedoring business was based at Millwall Dock. As we approached Millwall the mean and regimented streets opened out to our left. The Isle of Dogs was formed by a great loop in the river, like a horseshoe with its rounded side facing south towards Greenwich. The narrow neck of land to the north was breached by the West India Dock itself, which cut off the Isle of Dogs from the adjoining 'mainland'. In the centre of the island lay the two basins of the Millwall Dock: one lay north to south, opening into the West India Dock; the other lay east to west. It was at the western end of the latter basin that a swing bridge and a lock gave access to the river at Pier Head.

Completely surrounding the docks to the south, east and west lay the homes of the stevedores. Built on the original marsh, these houses were situated well below the level of the docks, so an unduly high tide always brought the risk of flooding. In the days before World War II, virtually the whole of the docks' workforce lived within walking or cycling distance of the 'Stones' – the hallowed ground where, twice daily, the hiring of men for work in the Millwall Docks took place. Canteens and amenities of any kind, apart from the most primitive of sanitary arrangements, were unknown, and the men arrived at work with their lunch in a knotted handkerchief. Tea was organized on a gang basis: it was brewed on board the ships and then passed to the men working in the holds or on the barges alongside.

The origins of our family stevedoring business were shrouded in obscurity. My great-great grandfather, also a John Hovey, was a waterman at Rotherhithe at the turn of the eighteenth and nineteenth centuries. His son, my great grandfather, also initially a waterman, subsequently founded the business. I was the fourth in direct line from him. Millwall Dock was opened in 1854, but by that time the Surrey Commercial Docks – the only other area in which our business used to operate – had already existed for half a century. It is a reasonable surmise that my great-grandfather, endowed with greater ambition and ability than his contemporaries, emerged as the leader of his colleagues, perhaps first as a foreman or manager and subsequently as an employer. Most if not all of the stevedoring businesses started in this way. The requirements in the early days were personal initiative and a willingness to take risks rather than capital: at that time the only material needs were a few ropes, chains, shackles and wires. This was an age before the telephone: even an office was a luxury. Success depended primarily on the availability of abundant casual labour. Piecework was the norm, and profitability depended solely on the contract which the master stevedore was able to strike with the shipowner and the amount of money per ton or per standard of timber that he was obliged to pay his men. The workers were, of course, only too well aware that, in a situation of casual labour, failure to work to an employer's satisfaction was likely to limit a docker's future work opportunities. Such a system earned London a reputation as one of the fastest-working ports in the world, far outstripping the continental rivals that have now surpassed it. Many fortunes were made by those who were lucky and astute enough to capitalise on the system. Yet the system brought with it the seeds of its own decay. There is no doubt that the memory of those days, passed down in a father-to-son industry, has been a potent factor in leading workers to suspect, and often resist, the post-war moves to modernise the docks.

The uncertainty of the dockers' employment and their total absence of security of earnings can perhaps be best illustrated by a story told of my grandfather (or perhaps my great-grandfather). The ships in the Scandinavian and Baltic trades, which were the speciality of the stevedores in the Millwall and Surrey Commercial Docks, being of approximately 1,000 tons burden and of no great draught, normally took on their pilot at Gravesend. He would bring them up river as far as Pier Head, where a dock pilot for Millwall Dock would bring the ship through the lock and into the dock. Should a ship drop anchor at Gravesend – which was not subject to a stevedoring contract – a number of rival master stevedores would board it there. My grandfather was, obviously, among them. Either by way of offering inducements to the master of the vessel, or by playing poker among themselves, the master stevedores would decide as the ship went further upriver who was to handle the discharge and loading. Such methods afforded no sense of security or continuity to the master stevedore, let alone to the men who depended on him each day for their sole means of livelihood.

Our family business grew and prospered, and my grandfather certainly became a well known figure in the City, where he and his fellow master stevedores haunted the *London Tavern* and struck the deals with shipowners on which their prosperity depended. But again the feeling of contrast was paramount: this time the contrast was between the plush saloons and riches of the City and the mean streets and grimy fastnesses of the docklands to which these men owed their riches.

But I should not be entirely negative about the pre-war docklands. Although my abiding memory of them is of drab and dismal surroundings, frequently cloaked in the obscure pallor of smoke and fog, and of wet pavements reflected in the fitful light of gas lamps under a seemingly near-incessant rain, these conditions did not subjugate the people. Cockneys are a resilient breed – Irish Cockneys perhaps particularly so. The origins of the docks, dug and worked by successive generations of the same families – the O'Learys, Dillons and Sheas – almost guaranteed a camaraderie in the face of exploitation, as well as an almost pathological loyalty based on the family and the gang. All this engendered a massive interdependence and unity, and above all a spirit of self-help and comradeship laced and lightened by an irrepressible sense of humour, the like of which is hard to find anywhere else. These attributes of the London dockers gave rise to the indomitable spirit that brought London through World War II. They have also given rise to the often near-blind solidarity which has played such an important part in the Port of London's subsequent decline.

2   *The aftermath of war*

It is clear that my early years were markedly sheltered from the realities of life in dockland. This was emphasised by my father's very natural wish that I should be educated in a manner which had not been available to him – at the age of 16 he had been required to enter his father's business. So I was sent away to boarding school in the country. The remembered links with dockland became even more tenuous. However, it was during my school days – no doubt through my study of history, in which I specialised – that my social conscience seems to have been stirred for the first time. Above all, the apparent accident of fate which was all that separated me from those nameless faces in their thousands who toiled in the holds or on the quays became more and more apparent to me. My mind still goes back to various pleasant Saturday afternoons at home (Saturday was then a full working day for the dockers). The peace of a summer's day might be broken by a thunderclap and there might be distant clouds in the north, towards where the docks lay. The telephone would ring, and my father's foreman would report: 'It's raining, guvnor'. 'Pay them off' was the invariable response. The ritual of cucumber sandwiches on the lawn would continue while, 10 miles away, hundreds of wet and disconsolate men were huddling in whatever shelter they could find, hoping that the rain would stop so that they could earn again.

My father wanted me to enter the diplomatic service. Many years later, in 1970, when I was leaving London for Southampton, the *Financial Times* wished to do a 'profile'. I was unwise enough to tell the reporter of my early training. Bearing in mind subsequent events, it is perhaps no surprise that the whole of his article centred embarrassingly on the theme that I had ended up doing 'something more diplomatic than the diplomatic'. Nevertheless, this early training of mine did set the scene for the future.

In 1941, having concluded my school career and having failed three times to win a history scholarship to Oxford, I, like most young men of my generation, volunteered for the armed services. I recall the summer's afternoon when, instead of playing cricket in the normal way, I and two of my schoolfriends paid an illicit visit to a recruiting office in Guildford. One of my friends joined the RAF, and was later killed in a bombing raid over Germany; the other joined the Army and was subsequently blown out of a tank in Normandy and grievously wounded. I joined the Navy.

That decision was to have a significant effect on the story of my life. When the war ended, the fact that I had seen so much of the sea and of seafarers – not to mention the ports at which they called – combined with a reluctance to re-enter the academic world (which I could have done), led me away from the diplomatic service and into the family business. After years of exposure to the bare facts of life, both good and bad, and to all sorts and conditions of mankind, I could not cut myself off from the *reality* which I had in a strange way come to love in favour of a more secluded academic life. It does my father the greatest credit that he did nothing to encourage me to enter his business. He made it very clear that he made no personal claim on me, and that the decision was very much mine. It is one on which I have reflected many times since. Friends used to ask me, particularly in the early years, how I could endure day after day the general rigours of dockland when I might have been enjoying the fleshpots of university, of some consular appointment, or of the City. But I have never regretted my choice, and have always felt that I was involved at the sharp end of something that, when the chips were down, mattered enormously. In short, it has been my privilege to have had the opportunity to better other peoples' lives, and to repay something of what I and my family owed to an industry which had given us so much.

I served in the Navy from 1941 to 1946, mostly – by choice – on small vessels. The only method of entry into the Navy in those times was, quite rightly, *via* the lower deck. This was perhaps the most formative period of my early career. To say that it was a make-or-break situation would be an understatement, and the culture shock I experienced as I went from a public-school environment to the mess deck of a cruiser was considerable. I was certainly pushed in at the deep end.

I shall never forget my first assignment. This was at a training establishment for new recruits at Fareham, where – at the age of barely 19 and due solely to the fact that I had been a sergeant in the school

Officers' Training Corps – I was put, without any rank whatsoever, in charge of 30 or so recruits. These men were aged up to 45 and were of all classes and conditions: some of them had done terms 'inside'. It was certainly a traumatic introduction to the ways of the world and one's fellow men, and was later to stand me in good stead in very many situations. At the end of the eight-week training course we had a party at the *Red Lion* in Fareham, and considerable quantities of beer flowed.

After a lifetime of work in industrial relations, it is still my conviction that I learned more about the management of men during my days at sea, particularly as a young sublieutenant on a trawler, than in all my days in the docklands. In a small ship, with perhaps four officers and 30 ratings, there is neither the time nor the inclination for ceremony: in a very real way you are 'all in one boat'. Yet in such circumstances the need for discipline and unquestioning obedience is paramount. But these come not from the King's Regulations or immaculate uniforms but from the genuine respect that individuals have for one another. I discovered that the path to really effective leadership is a narrow one. On the one side – and I have seen it all too often – are those who can stand on the bridge and shout the orders, but are unable to bring themselves down to the level of and into the hearts of those they command, and thus never get the best out of their people. On the other you find those who become so much identified with their people that the essential respect which is the foundation of leadership is lost. It is the best possible training in leadership to have to try to walk the tightrope between these two extremes.

I left the Navy in 1946 as a lieutenant. Without further ado I joined the family business. At the end of the war my father had turned this into a limited company, with himself as chairman. The other directors were all from the family: my father's two younger brothers, one of whom had had a distinguished war record with the Port Operating Regiment, and myself. I was wholly without experience, and so was given all the most humdrum clerical tasks.

The business continued to operate in Surrey Commercial Docks, but was mainly concentrated at Millwall. The old office at Pier Head had been destroyed during an enemy air-raid, along with the lock and entrance into the River Thames. Entrance for ships to Millwall was now from the east (or Blackwall) side of the Isle of Dogs *via* the West India Dock. Many of the century-old warehouses fronting the docks had also been destroyed; those that remained were dim, ill-lit places two storeys high, with barely eight feet of headroom, and interspaced at frequent intervals with metal stanchions to support the weight of the floor above. They had small doorways with platforms above, on which cargo could be landed for the top storey. These sheds were redolent of the Dickensian era. They had a section for casks and drums, one for bales of wool, one for coils of rope and wire, one for bales of carpet, and one for piece goods of every shape and size. Every package had to be manhandled individually onto a hand barrow and trundled up onto the quayside, where it was tipped out onto a cargo board. This would be lifted by a set of wires hooked to the corners and attached by a single ring to the hook of a crane or winch, and then hoisted on board. Then the contents of the board would be broken down and carried or manhandled piece by piece into the furthermost recesses of the hold. It was a slow process, labour-intensive to the last degree. The opportunity for injury was ever-present, and the strain of, say, humping countless bags of sugar that each weighed a couple of hundred weight, day after day and year after year, inevitably took its toll in life and limb as men approached their early and middle fifties. Another frequently handled commodity was asbestos, and it was a common sight to see the ill ventilated cargo spaces full of asbestos dust as the holds were swept after a consignment had been discharged. Some 20 years later it became generally known that the lethal disease of asbestosis could result from inhaling this dust, and men who had handled this cargo regularly became its innocent victims. In short, the life of a stevedore or docker was hard, dirty and often dangerous.

Since the old office on Pier Head had been destroyed, the Port of London Authority, which owned the docks, provided us with temporary accommodation. This consisted of a very basic wooden shed, to serve as an office for at most two or three clerks, plus a gear store, which was little bigger. The latter contained the accoutrements of the master stevedore's trade: chains, wires, ropes, shackles and all the other paraphernalia that enabled us to carry on the business.

Immediately I was struck by another of those contrasts, the recognition of which has done so much to condition my life. My family had prospered over the generations from the fruits of their labours in the docks, and yet in terms of ownership they were insignificant. The giant Port of London Authority, inheritors of the commercial speculators of the nineteenth century who had built the enclosed docks, were the owners and operators of the port. So far as Millwall Dock was concerned, they carried out all the operations on the quay, were responsible for all the warehouses, provided all the cranes, and organised the coming and going of vessels and the berthing of those vessels in their docks. Their headquarters at Trinity Square in the City, from the portico of which Father Neptune pointed his trident meaningfully down-river, was a building of imperial magnificence – indeed, it represented the hub of a commercial empire. Under its aegis a hierarchy of dock superintendents, dock masters, traffic officers and engineers supervised and regulated the authority's affairs from Tower Bridge to Tilbury; and, on the river itself, there was a separate division responsible for maintaining the navigation of the tideway. The other great vested interest concerned the shipowners, for whom the docks had been built and on whom their prosperity depended. And yet, with the sole exception of the West India and London docks, in which the Port of London Authority undertook the discharging and loading of all vessels, this most important and in many ways most lucrative part of the operations was performed by neither the authority nor, with a few notable exceptions, by the shipowners but by a select band of master-stevedore companies, most of which were family concerns, based on the time-honoured principle of father-to-son inheritance. This was of course hardly surprising, bearing in mind that many of the master-stevedore firms had sprung from the ranks of the stevedores themselves. It is not surprising that, as a breed, the master stevedores were independent, tough and resilient to a degree; and, although they undoubtedly exploited the labour force, this was no more than the common ethic of the day. To their credit, many of them worked alongside their men, and some had acquired Stevedore's Tickets, of which they were justly proud. Above all, within the limits of the casual system, they knew their men and were – albeit often grudgingly – respected by them.

But we still have to account for the fact that both the mighty Port of London Authority and the shipowners – the groups with whom the real power lay – chose to accept a system in which entrepreneurs or middlemen could control the fulcrum of the business, the loading and discharge of vessels. The answer must lie in the prevailing Victorian attitude of *laissez faire,* which encouraged the system to develop, and particularly in the attitude of the shipowners who, just as the master stevedores could exploit a situation in which the number of daily labourers available was greater than the number that could be employed, were themselves able to exploit the often cut-throat competition between the various master stevedores so as to secure the fastest despatch at the lowest possible cost. Above all, this policy meant that as soon as each of his ships had sailed the shipowner had little further responsibility to the master stevedore, much less to the labourers who had actually worked the vessel. The shipowner was thus able to distance himself from the dirty end of the business and, if not satisfied in terms of either performance or price, could always change his master stevedore. Certainly the emergence and predominance of the master stevedore was a direct product of the casual system of employment. It seemed quite clear to me that, if one recognized the evils of the casual system, it was particularly appropriate that a master stevedore should play a central part in removing that system.

The nature of the organisation of the men in the docks had its roots in the days of sail. With the exception of the lightermen, who earned their livelihood handling barges in the docks and on the river, and of the tally clerks, who had the specialist task of counting and checking the cargoes against the ships' manifests, the workforce was divided into dockers and stevedores. Historically the dockers (or 'whites', as they were known from the colour of their union cards, and who were eventually to be absorbed into the Transport and General Workers Union) had worked on the quays and in the warehouses of the independent dock companies; many were subsequently employed by the Port of London Authority. The stevedores (or 'blues'), with whom my family company worked exclusively, undertook all work aboard vessels, and were acknowledged experts in the safe loading and stowage of the cargoes. This was a life-and-death affair, particularly in the days of sail, when a ship caught in a squall or by a sudden change in the direction of the wind could be subject to violent movement of every kind: should the stowage of the cargo be less than perfect it might shift in the hold, with almost-certain disaster as a result. The stevedores' pride in their work and the expertise which this engendered persisted long after the demise of the sailing ships. The art of stowage – for it was an art – was passed down from father to son within the stevedoring families.

In the days of piecework, before and after World War II, this art achieved a new significance. Purpose-built ships for the carriage of motor cars had yet to be built, and so exports of these were invariably combined with general cargo. The optimum use of space in the holds and the consequent maximum earnings from piecework which this entailed required the creation of a 'level' in the hold on which motor cars could be loaded and pushed into the wings of the ship. Cases and cartons of every size and description, barrels and drums, reels of cable, iron bars, bales of wool and commodities of all sorts would be used to form this level, and by and large the only tools available were a crowbar and the ubiquitous stevedore's hook. It was a good example of the advantage of a financial incentive, although frequently it was of doubtful benefit to the cars!

A particular speciality of the stevedore was the handling of timber. The London timber trade had historically been centred on the vast complex of docks and canals which lay on the south side of the Thames between Bermondsey and Rotherhithe, and which came to be known as the Surrey Commercial Docks. The first of these enclosed docks, the Great Howland Dock as it was then known, was built at the beginning of the nineteenth century as a haven where sailing ships could seek shelter from the exposed tidal waters of the river; for this purpose it was surrounded by a screen of poplar trees. Later it was rechristened the Greenland Dock, and subsequent names, such as Canada Dock, Quebec Dock, Brunswick Yard, Finland Dock and Baltic Dock, bear witness to the worldwide nature of the timber trade. Our company had carried on business in the Surrey Commerical Dock since the 1870s, although the firm's physical presence there was even less than in Millwall Dock across the river. We had the smallest of wooden huts in Station Yard and a primitive shed alongside to house the indispensable steel chains, hooks and wires. But, more importantly, our centre of operations here lay within hailing distance of the 'Stones'.

The importance of this ritual cannot be over-emphasised. Much has been written of its iniquity; indeed, its basic ethic of 'every man for himself and the devil take the hindmost', on which so much of Victorian

17

prosperity was built, was the factor which eventually proved unacceptable in more enlightened times and so finally led to its overthrow. I have already described how the master stevedores, each in bitter competition with the next, would secure a contract, albeit tenuous, for the handling of a ship. That contract would specify the rate per ton of general cargo (or per standard of timber) that the shipowner was prepared to pay, and it was for the master stevedore to keep his labour bill as low as possible in order to make a decent profit. Moreover, he had to ensure that the ship was turned round expeditiously if he was to satisfy the shipowner and so secure further contracts.

Each master stevedore employed on a permanent basis a number of foremen. One of their duties was to secure the gangs of men required to work on the incoming vessels. (In the early years the master stevedores presumably performed this task themselves.) On a typical morning as many as 15–20 vessels could be expected in the Surrey Commercial Docks, and for each of these there would be a foreman presenting himself on the 'Stones' beneath a sign, denoting the name of his firm, on the oak palings edging the road. Opposite the contending foremen the mass of the stevedores currently without work assembled. With their union cards – the necessary passport to employment – held aloft, they would 'shape' towards the foreman and job of their choice. The men as a rule worked in 'gangs' of 12–13, often based on a family unit. In addition there were individuals who preferred to be 'floaters'. Some gangs were accustomed to 'following' certain employers who were able, because of the nature of their contracts, to offer them continuity of work. Other, and these included many of the ablest, were 'floating gangs' who offered their services to the highest bidder.

In this situation it was not what but whom you knew that mattered. In the days when handling equipment was basic and cheap, so that the speed of work was determined by the number of men and their collective muscle-power, the master stevedore who could produce the most, best and fastest workers aboard an owner's vessel was certain of success.

In these circumstances it was the events preceding the 'call', rather than the 'call' itself, which were significant. On the evening before a ship's arrival (news of which would be obtained from contacts at Gravesend) the foreman would busy himself making discreet visits to the Bermondsey pubs in which the stevedores gathered; in the days after the telephone became available he could instead indulge in a series of clandestine phone calls to the various 'gangers' he knew. His aim was, of course, to be able to report to his 'guvnor' at eight o'clock the next morning that the ship was fully manned by first-class gangs.

It was against this background that what was often the charade of the 'call' took place. Those who had been contacted beforehand immediately shaped for the employer who had engaged them. Those outside the favoured circles sought work in vain unless, on a rare occasion, there were so many incoming vessels that employers were obliged to take on all comers. This practice, together with the piecework system which guaranteed high pay for high performance, resulted in a speed of work by the best of the 'blue-eyed gangs' which has rarely if ever been surpassed; but its manifest unfairness, especially when combined with the bribery and corruption which could so easily occur, brought its nemesis. It is no exaggeration to say that the best jobs frequently went to those who were prepared to buy the foreman the most pints of beer in the pub the evening before.

A visit to the Surrey Docks in those days was something to savour. As soon as you left the mean streets of Bermondsey and passed through the wooden stockade which enclosed the docks, the sights and smells were only of timber. It was as though you had entered a different world, a cross between a pine forest and some gigantic builders' yard. There was timber everywhere of every conceivable shape and size: giant mahogany logs from West Africa; made-to-measure sleepers and sturdy 12-by-4s from Vancouver; the battens and boards that were the staple of the Baltic Trades. The ships themselves were laden to bridge-level with deck cargoes of timber, and on the open quays vast stacks of timber, house-high, awaited collection by merchants' lorries. To reach a ship you had to traverse a succession of deep alleyways, dark gloomy places beyond the reach of the sun but with a pungent aroma redolent of the pine forests of Sweden or Finland. Here and there, vast open-sided warehouses gave shelter to those classes of timber which could be damaged by exposure to the weather. One area of water was given over to a mass of floating timber where huge logs from West Africa were deliberately saturated. Elsewhere the Port of London Authority stacked acre upon acre of logs in the open air for seasoning, each cut lengthwise into a dozen or so planks, separated by battens to allow the circulation of air.

Even the waters were covered in timber, lost overboard during the discharge of vessels or from overladen barges as they traversed the docks. Such 'dunnage' became the property of the insurers, who employed the Port of London Authority to collect it. From time to time it would be sold to the highest bidder.

Most of the timber was discharged into barges and then conveyed by the lighterage companies' small tugs in strings of several barges at a time to riverside wharves, or up the inland canals to customers' premises, where it could be more easily discharged. The portion brought ashore deserves special mention. A ship loaded bridge-high with a deck cargo of 12-by-4s would berth alongside an empty quay. The first planks would be made up into setts and landed on the quayside using the ship's winches. Frequently, however, they were buried in the depths of the deck cargo. In this case the planks would be passed down one by one, and as the stack on the quay rose it soon became possible to construct a simple gangplank from the top of the deck cargo to the stack on the shore. Over this plank, perhaps 20 ft above water-level, the stevedores carried the heavy planks on their shoulders one or two at a time – sometimes at a walk, sometimes at a run – and deposited them on the ever-rising stack. To protect their shoulders the lumpers, as they were called, wore special leather shoulderpads; the customary cloth cap gave some measure of protection to the head. Finally, after days of labour, the holds would be empty, and the ship would emerge as a thing of beauty, of masts and spars, a creature of the sea. As she threaded her way through the accumulated dunnage to the river and the sea, she left behind her scores of laden barges and vast edifices of timber on the quayside, towering above the timber-strewn waters where she had lain.

Today, the Surrey Commercial Docks are no more, and a vast housing estate broods over what remains of the docks and waterways. It has fallen victim to a complete change in the pattern of trade. Timber is no longer carried in single pieces, but instead is packaged in the country of origin into huge units which can be lifted with modern machinery or placed in containers. The ships which carry it are far too large and deep-draughted to manoeuvre through the narrow locks and cuttings of the old docks. With the passing of the docks has vanished a way of life and indeed a whole community. The humour and independence of the Old Kent Road are immortalised in song, and there is no doubt that the free-for-all which the dockland life represented produced characteristics of rugged interdependence and irrepressible cheerfulness which represented all that was best in Cockney London. They have fallen victim to the inevitability of change, but we should mourn their passing. Those people were the children of their age; the working practices they tolerated were an incarnation of *laissez faire* and the very antithesis of the social ethic that produced the welfare state and the planned economy. Yet the Surrey Docks provided employment for thousands of Londoners, and above all bred a sturdy independence based on the fact that, in such a system, only the man prepared to work and to fight for himself would survive. These times were a romantic and valuable part of our history, but their passing was as inevitable as the next high water. Mourn as we may, we might as well regret the passing of the dinosaurs. And, as I have said, the system under which these human beings had to operate was a brutal one.

When I first came to Millwall, my father ensured that I should absorb the character of dockland at first hand. Our family had always had closer and better relationships with their workers, within the limits of a casual system, than was then the norm. My first mentor was Frank Nightingale, a devoted old servant, then approaching his seventies, who had given a lifetime of service ‑ as indeed had his father before him – to my family. Frank was a man of few words but much authority. He was accustomed to dealing with all sorts of people with firmness and decisiveness, but never in all my dealings with him did I hear even the mildest obscenity cross his lips.

Frank, with his gentle voice, his cloth cap and his red kerchief, was a gentleman of the docklands. When he died, his funeral procession stopped at the bridge where our old office at Pier Head had been so that stevedores (in their hundreds), office staff, masters and officers of ships and, of course, the master stevedores themselves could pay their last respects. The *Weekly Boat,* Swedish Lloyd's regular weekly passenger steamer berthed in Millwall Docks, blew her whistle in a very genuine mark of respect.

Frank confirmed for me, I think, what I had already learned in the Navy, that every man should be valued for what he makes of his life, rather than for the particular calling to which destiny has assigned him. I have always believed in treating all people, high or low, with the same basic consideration, and any judgement that one must sometimes make has to be based on what that person has done with the opportunities given to him or her. I can honestly say that, in 40 years' connection with dockland, I have received nothing but kindness and respect from the individuals working under me, and I can scarcely recall any occasion when the inescapable fact that I am my father's son has occasioned any bitterness or, indeed, done anything except improve our ability to relate to each other.

Our family business at Millwall was historically centred around two Swedish shipping companies in the general cargo trade; Swedish Lloyd was based in Gothenburg and the Svea Company in Stockholm. We had been fortunate enough to have contracts with these companies for many years. Although the shipowners could have broken the contracts at any time, they had never had cause to do so. This gave our business the advantage of a good deal of continuity and alleviated some of the more blatant evils of the casual system, as we were able to employ some 15 – 20 gangs on a semi-permanent basis. This arrangement enabled us to get to know many of the men as individuals, and in some cases their families as well. We were thus in the unusual position of having reasonably close employer-employee relationships – something normally impossible in the casual system. I am sure that it was this aspect that convinced me, from my earliest association with the docks, that the concept of a tightly knit working unit, in which master and man could cooperate fully to their common benefit, was the most important objective for the future.

One of the by-products of this kind of relationship, although it was certainly not confined to our firm, was the annual beano. This traditionally took place on the sovereign's official birthday, which was always a holiday in the docks. Charabancs were hired and managers, foremen, gangers and those men who traditionally 'followed' us were transported to Margate or some other south-coast watering place. These journeys were festive in the extreme, with many stops for the consumption of alchohol. In my grandfather's day he took the precaution of going separately with his chauffeur and Rolls Royce to Margate, only then joining in the revelry. No doubt this degree of independence also made it easier for him to make good his escape should the situation require. Such events belong very much to past generations, and may be frowned on in today's climate, but they provided an opportunity for employers and employees to come together and communicate informally, often to mutual benefit.

Another example of the dockers' 'togetherness' was the annual pilgrimage to the hop-fields of Kent for a working holiday. Whole gangs of men, with their families, would travel together, and the benefits of the chance to cement the working relationship while at the same time having a complete change of atmosphere, enjoy the fresh air of Kent and continue to earn meanwhile can well be imagined.

Festivities were not confined to the men – far from it. The social life enjoyed by the employers and managers in Millwall Dock was a hectic one. On any one week our company could be handling as many as 7 – 8 small Swedish ships. Presiding like a mother hen over her chicks was the Swedish Lloyd passenger steamer, lying at her berth regularly from Monday to Saturday, when she sailed to pick up her passengers for Gothenburg at the Tilbury landing stage. She had first-class facilities for passengers, and it was the custom of her master to invite his fellow-masters from the other ships in port to lunch with him during the week. It is hardly surprising that others wished to return the compliment, and it was not unusual for at least four such luncheons to be held during the working week. To some of these would be invited representatives of the ship's agents in the City, and they would often bring a selection of the more important cargo shippers. The Port Authority was often represented, occasionally by the dock superintendent but more frequently by the dock master who, presumably because of his maritime background, was felt more able to compete with the sometimes excessive hospitality of his fellow mariners. To all of these luncheons the master stevedore was invited and, if he wished to further his business, it was unwise of him to refuse. It was thus commonplace for the men, working in their barges between the vessel and quay, to see the 'guvnors', in their topcoats and bowler hats, walking up the gangway at noon or thereabouts, and later, around 4.30pm, in varying degrees of instability, leaving by the same route and past the same men. It says much for the innate common decency of the average docker that such circumstances did not as a rule provoke any other emotion than (I am sure) a great deal of envy, but I often wonder to what extent excesses of this kind did in fact set the scene for some of the industrial problems that occurred in later years.

Such was the nature of the industry which I came to know immediately after World War II. Its methods and attitudes basically unchanged since the beginning of the century, it epitomised both the best and the worst aspects of Victorian society. At its best, the way the work had been performed had gained for Britain a reputation for industry and expertise unrivalled in the civilized world, and this had helped London to achieve its position as the unquestioned leader among the ports of Europe. The other side of the coin was that the system which had produced all this industry was grounded in insecurity, lack of responsibility, exploitation and frequently corruption of the worst kind. The changes which were to come were inevitable as, in the wake of two world wars, social attitudes and human expectations shifted. The tragedy is that, in the removal of the undoubted evils, so much of what was good and profitable was lost as well.

3   The first stirrings of change

I have described the situation as it was when I joined my family company in 1946. This was essentially a time of change, a time when the crying need for change and the will to achieve it had come together. Above all, the casual nature of employment was being called into question. This was nothing new – indeed, the iniquities of the system had been highlighted and challenged since the beginning of the century, particularly during the period between the two world wars. The central question was whether, in order to ensure security to the dock workers and a sufficiency of labour to the employers, dock workers should be registered, with only registered men being allowed to do the work. Opinion on all sides was divided. The trade unions in general, and Ernest Bevin in particular, engaged in a long battle to achieve registration, but were resisted not only by the employers but in many instances also by their own members, who were reluctant to give up the total freedom of action which the casual system conferred. For example, under the casual system, if after a week's profitable employment in the Surrey Commercial Docks a man chose to spend a couple of days at the Brighton Races, that was his absolute prerogative, and if the shipowner's vessel was delayed as a consequence, that was just too bad. Almost all of the shipowners and master stevedores opposed registration bitterly, on the grounds that it would limit the inexhaustible supply of unskilled labour available because of the substantial unemployment that prevailed between the wars. There were several notable exceptions to the general rule. Having started at an early age as messenger boys, about half of the Port of London Authority's men were permanently employed, and a limited number of shipowners and master stevedores engaged a small number of dockworkers on a 'permanent' or 'preferred' basis. But these were very much in a minority – although they were to pave the way for eventual decasualisation. Indeed, it is of interest that Scruttons, the largest of the master-stevedore companies, actually offered permanent employment to their casuals before World War I. It is a sad commentary on employer-employee relations of the day that the *Daily Herald* described the offer (which was rejected by the unions) as 'taking the dockers into slavery'! The strength of the opposition was such that, in spite of several government enquiries, notably the Shaw Report of 1920, nothing was achieved. At the outbreak of war in 1939 the situation was little changed from that at the end of World War I.

World War II changed the whole pattern of our national life. One of the by-products was the sweeping away of all further resistance to the registration of labour, and eventual decasualisation was the inevitable result. Beleaguered and beset by blockade from without, Britain's maritime links with what remained of the free world became its lifeline: the expeditious handling of the ships that brought in the cargoes to feed our people and sustain our war effort was paramount. The convoys (in the protection of which I was in a small way involved while in the Navy) were in some cases shattered and invariably diminished by the time they reached our battle-scarred ports. Common sense therefore dictated that a sufficient, well organised and disciplined labour force had to be available to deal with those ships which beat the blockade.

The other decisive factor was the availability of labour. There had been years of unemployment and reliance on the ready availability of a pool of men. Now there came call-up to the services, including the creation of special Port Operating regiments largely staffed by dockers and stevedores; these distinguished themselves particularly during the invasions of Africa, Italy and Northwestern Europe. There was thus a shortage of labour in the docks, an intolerable situation in time of war. Ernest Bevin – who before he achieved pre-eminence in the trade union movement, had himself been a representative of Bristol dockworkers and had thereby acquired first-hand experience of the casual system – had by now become Churchill's Minister of Labour, and he proceeded forthwith with compulsory registration. This was accomplished in two ways. For the ports of Mersey and Clyde, which were of prime importance during the war and were already controlled by the Ministry of War Transport, registers of dock workers were compiled and the ports put effectively under the direction of port directors appointed by the government. It is interesting that both managers and men were sent from London to Liverpool, Bristol and the Clyde; the principle of consultation with the trade unions was enshrined in all these arrangements. For the remaining ports Bevin went further. Not only were the men registered and given the sole right to dockers' work but they were to have the protection of a newly created National Dock Labour Corporation – the precursor of the National Dock Labour Board (see below). This had a chairman and a vice-chairman appointed by the government, but the principle of joint control of the industry was introduced by the additional appointment to the corporation of an equal number of representatives (initially three) from each of the two major interest groups, the employers and the trade unions.

These arrangements served the purpose of providing a reliable and efficient service in time of war – although it has to be admitted in passing that they did not prevent strikes and disputes, of which there were many. We should perhaps not be surprised that men who for years had felt themselves treated as chattels, but who had now suddenly been presented with evidence that they were important to the community and the nation, should react by wielding a power which had never before been so effective, the power to withdraw their labour.

The immediate post-war political climate likewise accelerated change and, especially throughout the services, there was a very natural reluctance to return to pre-war situations which were identified with hierarchical or autocratic institutions of any kind. The British have never taken particularly well to an excess of discipline, and there is no doubt that generally felt war-weariness also contributed to the reaction against regimentation and direction from above. The individual once again reasserted his or her prerogatives: it was in every sense the 'age of the common man'. This was felt even more keenly in the port transport industry because so many of the men had been enlisted into the Port Operating regiments and had been subject to military discipline. On demobilisation the rugged individuality of the dock worker reasserted itself, and gave additional impetus to the drive to end the casual system.

Bevin, although by this time elevated to the post of Foreign Secretary in the Attlee government, had by no means abandoned his interest in the docks, and it was his influence within the government which was largely responsible for the continued pressure to end the casual system. After the experience of World War II, none of the parties – government, employers or trade unions – showed any wish to return to the free-for-all of pre-war years. In view of the continuing inability of the two sides of the industry to agree in the National Joint Council a scheme for the registration of labour and the provision of fall-back pay when no work was available in ports throughout the country, the Labour government in June, 1947, acted on its own authority and established the National Dock Labour Board under the aegis of the Dockworkers' (Regulation of Employment) Scheme.

Thus was accomplished the first major change in the structure of the industry. For the first time the men were to enjoy a form of security protected by law. They were no longer to be wholly subject to the vagaries of wind and weather, and the National Dock Labour Board was required to pay them a fall-back payment whether work was available or not. Above all, the principle of joint control of the industry on a 50/50 basis, at both national and local levels, was officially imposed.

The second major step to complete the decasualisation process was not to take place for a further two decades, during which the industry suffered the greatest number of disputes, and lost the greatest number of man-hours in strikes, in its history, Thus, as so often in Britain's history, the result of a far-reaching and laudable social advance was to whet peoples' appetites and increase their expectations for more, rather than to elicit their gratitude, allay their fears and enlist their cooperation.

Our family business, which was increasingly restricted to Millwall Docks, was probably less affected by the creation of the National Dock Labour Board than most. Our daily requirement for men did not fluctuate too wildly, and the principal change was that the men now possessed registration books which they presented to their employer on engagement for a particular job. The employer stamped these for every half day's work, and at the end of each day compiled lists of the men's earnings which were taken to the local office of the board. Those men who did not obtain work on the 'call' – which continued as before – presented their registration books at the board office and were rewarded by an attendance stamp or 'bomper'. This had to be applied for twice a day for as long as the man had no work; if work was on offer elsewhere in the Port of London the man was duty-bound to accept it. At the end of each week the board collated the men's wages and attendance money and paid them in cash.

There is no doubt that, for the vast majority of the men who worked in the docks, the Dock Labour Scheme was an unqualified blessing. For the employers the benefits were less evident. Certainly, in the situation of full employment which existed for the first two decades after the end of the war, the scheme guaranteed a permanently available source of labour. What it did not do was secure quality. This still depended on the old methods of the 'call' but, if insufficient 'regular' gangs were available on any particular day, the employer was obliged to receive men allocated by the board from any sector of the Port of London where a surplus of labour existed. Thus on any given day at Millwall short-handed gangs might have to be made up by men coming from London Docks, the Royal Docks or the Surrey Commerical Docks: in each case there was an hour's travelling time involved. The journey from Tilbury took even longer – three hours – and it was always a bone of contention among employers as to whether it was worth their while to accept these men. Because the unions forbade short-handed gangs to work, and because the men allocated from elsewhere were rarely used to or had their hearts in the work, delays and frustrations were considerable. Such allocations were made on a daily basis, yet the consequent delays could account for half a day's production. It is perhaps no wonder that the employers, ourselves included, were quickly disillusioned by the administrative deficiencies of the scheme.

The other major problem surrounding the scheme was the question of discipline. This quickly became apparent. Discipline was governed wholly by the board, which was itself established on the principle of joint control. Offences such as bad timekeeping could be dealt with by the employer, but the man could and did invariably appeal to the board, who would hear representations from both the employers and the trade-union officers acting on the man's behalf. The maximum punishment was five days' suspension from the scheme – so that the man was deprived of a week's earnings – and this was only after much delay and on the assumption that the man's appeal was turned down. More serious offences, including those for which dismissal was sanctioned, went before the local board, where the decision was made on a joint basis. It swiftly became apparent that the trade-union official, often elected by his members, had been placed in an impossible position – how could he legislate against them? The chairman had no casting vote and so stalemate on a 50/50 basis became the order of the day. In all my years in Millwall I can recall dismissal from the industry, the ultimate sanction, being sustained only in the event of criminal conviction – either for theft or for assault and battery. Thus the employers had moved overnight from a situation in which they could simply not engage potential troublemakers to one in which they were legally bound to engage them and unable to dismiss them. It is no wonder that they were unhappy.

The other important change was that the board became the man's nominal and legal employer. The results of this change are more difficult to quantify. Although the man's wages were subsequently recovered from the employer and the shipowner by a levy, they were paid by the board. There is no doubt that this weakening of the links between the employer and those who worked for him contributed to the disaffection of the next few years. The man's loyalty became divided between his trade union, his employer of the day and the board, and was consequently diluted.

For the industry, the period from 1945 to 1965 in many ways represented the period of half-light at the beginning of the new day. With the registration of dock workers and the establishment of the National Dock Labour Board, the first stop towards decasualisation had been taken. Traditional links with the employer – based, it is true, on exploitation and often corruption – had been broken; they were not to be re-established, with the allocation of permanent workers to employers, for another 20 years. During this time all parties suffered. The traditional excellence of work in our ports declined to the point at which valuable trade began increasingly to be lost to Continental ports which were not only able to offer shift systems (not available in Britain) but surpassed our ports in excellence and in competitive cost. The inevitable result was a dramatic reduction in the register of dock workers. The introduction of new technology reduced it further. The net effect was that a nationwide register of approximately 100,000 when first created had diminished to approximately 12,000 by the time I left the industry at the end of 1985.

One other deficiency deserves a mention. As I have said earlier, while the master stevedores employed the men on the ship the Port of London Authority employed the men to receive the cargo on the quay. The Port of London Authority was more dependent on allocated men than we were, and it was frequently the case that we had a ship gang which was unable to work because the authority had no shore gang to receive the cargo. Less frequently, a shore gang stood idle because we had no ship gang. In either event, labour was wasted and valuable turnaround time lost while allocated men travelled from Tilbury or elsewhere.

The National Dock Labour Board was not concerned with industrial relations, which remained the prerogative of the National Joint Council for the Port Transport Industry. Under the council, various local joint committees were set up for the ports. London, because of its size, boasted a Port of London Executive Committee (also jointly constituted) and separate local joint committees for the ocean trades, the Port of London Authority, the riverside and the lighterage interests. (I subsequently became Joint Chairman of the London Ocean Trades Group Joint Committee.) The ocean-trades committee in its turn appointed a piece-work subcommittee to fix piece-work rates and to authorise area committees to meet aboard any ships where there were problems and difficulties with the piece-work rates.

These area committees provided perhaps the finest school of industrial relations one could hope to have been trained in. Those who participated over the years included many of the trade-union leaders and some of the employers who were subsequently to make their mark on the industry. The committees were joint, and in every case a joint decision had to be made. It needed a brave trade unionist (and there were many) to decide in favour of the employer. Much more frequently employers, under pressure from ship-owners to get their ships away, conceded to the men. Piece-work rates were traditionally fixed on the basis of providing a reasonable return for a reasonable rate of output, and it was always assumed that men were able to work without impediment of any kind. Stoppages for which the men were not responsible – such as rain, waiting for the Port Authority's labour to arrive, or covering the holds with beams and hatches – were compensated for by the payment of one or more hours of daywork to be added to the piece-work bill. The purpose of the area committee was to assess the degree of hindrance suffered by the men because of the special circumstances of the job. The workers would then be awarded a number of hours' daywork, or indeed a lump sum for the completion of the job.

The inspection committees frequently had an unpleasant as well as an onerous task. For example, many ships of the 'tween-deck' variety were built with long alleyways, extending perhaps 50–60 ft on either side of the engine-room casing. If space was at a premium, it was the custom to fill these alleyways from ceiling to deckhead with cargo – anything from lengths of timber to bales of hardboard. Much of this would have to be handled piece by piece the full length of the alleyway, and in conditions made much worse by the heat from the engine room. An added complication was the existence of bunker spaces for the carriage of fuel in emergency. These were likewise sometimes filled with cargo, which had to be manhandled through small openings (sometimes as small as two feet by four feet) in the steel structure. Such jobs frequently qualified for lump-sum payments.

Another frequent chore for the area committees concerned wet salted hides imported raw for tanning. Quite often the hides became infested by maggots during the voyage. The traditional docker's defence was a bucket of water and plenty of carbolic soap. The stench which the examining committee – and the dockers – had to endure could be overpowering, and the general unpleasantness, if proven, was held to justify a substantial reward.

The most serious claims facing the committee were those of salvage. When a ship had been in collision or on fire, or a hold had been flooded, or it was necessary to discharge a hold in order to secure the ship's safety, a claim for salvage was inevitable. Perhaps naturally, the men did not hesitate to extort the last possible penny in a situation in which they knew that the owner depended on them to remove or reduce the threat of loss to his vessel, and that anyway in all probability it would be the insurers rather than the owner who would eventually foot the bill.

It is perhaps appropriate here to step aside and take a closer look at the piece-work, or payment-by-results, system.

There is no doubt that in the unadulterated casual system which existed before World War II, and in times of endemic unemployment, the system produced rates of working which have never been surpassed. It gave a great deal of freedom to the individual, who was free to work as quickly or as slowly as he wished. The pressures of unemployment and the employers' ability to hire and fire as they pleased invariably resulted in high outputs and commensurately high earnings. In the post-war situation, once a much greater measure of security had been given to the men by registration and the 'fall-back', and with over-full employment, the cutting edge of the piece-work system was considerably blunted.

Added to this were the substantial organisational delays imposed by the Dock Labour Scheme, which made it difficult for the piece-worker to achieve the uninterrupted flow of work on which he depended. It was therefore no surprise that pressure rose for the piece-work content of the pay bill to be boosted by daywork payments to make the resultant earnings more attractive.

At first these payments were legitimate, to compensate for delays caused by weather or for other reasons genuinely outside the man's control, but increasingly they were used by employers to boost the mens' earnings artificially, as only the offer of high earnings could retain the rates of output at the pre-war level to which the shipowners had become accustomed. The men were, of course, swift to seize on this weakness. Particularly when dealing with private master stevedores, they demanded the payment of daywork: more and more, this blackmail money had to be paid if a reasonable output was to be guaranteed. In the late 1950s and the 1960s things got so bad that, in many cases, piece-work gangs – whose earnings should have been related solely to their efforts – were not prepared to start work at all until the employer had conceded a minimum payment for the day. Any piece-work which the man might subsequently earn would then be added to this already adequate minimum.

The other major factor which called into question the piece-work system was the introduction of the calculation of piece-work on the basis of 'weight or measurement, whichever is the greater'. This came about largely because of the great quantities of high-measurement cargo, such as Bailey bridging, that had had to be shipped out during the war. It was of course perfectly fair that, for example, cartons of cornflakes should not be paid on the same per-ton weight basis as ingots of metal. The purpose of 'weight or measurement' payment was to try to equate the effort required and to adjust the earnings accordingly. But there were problems. For example, a cargo might consist of motor cars. These required only to be pushed along the quays and into their stowage on the ship, but afforded, because of their large measurement, earnings out of all proportion to the effort required. The manifest unfairness of this – other gangs might be loading cement and being paid far less – led to the accusation, often justifiable, that the best jobs were reserved for the 'blue-eyed boys'.

The accelerating erosion of the piece-work system had many other undesirable facets. Perhaps the worst was the blackmail which could be exerted on employers and shipowners. A fairly typical incident concerned a Greek vessel on charter to one of our Swedish owners. This ship was in Millwall Dock, discharging reels of newsprint for one of the national dailies. The vessel was unusual in that an additional discharging point had been created in one very large hold by the simple if unusual expedient of cutting a large hole in the main deck. Through this hole, probably 12 – 14 ft square, the heavy reels of newsprint had to be hoisted by crane, care having to be taken not to damage them by contact with the razor-sharp metal edges of the hole. It was a difficult job, and the men certainly deserved a lump-sum payment. The inevitable area committee was convened. A generous award, amply compensating the men for the additional time and care needed, was made, but the men, protected from dismissal by the Dock Labour Scheme and their confidence bolstered by the unusual nature of the job, refused to accept the offer. In such circumstances – the award having been made by a committee representing employers, shipowners and trade unions – the employers were expected to stand firm and not to countenance any further extra payment. In this case the master stevedore did so, as did the chartering shipowner; but the owner of the vessel, seeing the possibility of delay and consequent loss, despatched an emissary to the docks with a fistful of fivers to distribute among the men. The next we knew was that the cargo was ashore and the ship had sailed. There were many such instances and, although it was rare for them to be so blatant, they served not only to discredit employers and trade unions alike but also to drive yet another nail into the coffin of the piece-work system.

To make matters worse, the employers' endless efforts to make a failing piece-work system work not only occupied a disproportionate part of their time – giving away a pound here and half-a-crown there to boost the mens' earnings, time which could have been much better spent on constructive forward management – but it also involved a practice of giving 'backhanders'. This practice had the unofficial blessing of all parties in the industry, yet it nevertheless verged on the corrupt. One of my first jobs in Millwall Dock was, on the completion of every vessel, to grease the palms to varying degrees of the masters, mates and ships' clerks, the employees of the cargo-superintending firms who were responsible for making the official returns of cargo handled to the owners.

It was a job I profoundly disliked, and at which I was disgracefully incompetent, sometimes to the extent of giving the varying amounts to the wrong people.

Only afterwards did I learn that our own foremen and sometimes the gangers received similar payments from the very individuals I had been paying. So the cash was in many cases going full circle. In this way the wheels of commerce were oiled, and a good many people were kept happy, but it was not something of which I was proud. It engendered in me an increasing distaste for the piece-work system. This distaste was to be significant at a later stage.

The situation in the 1950s and early 1960s in London and in many other ports was thus:

- the process of decasualisation, demanded not only by social conscience but now also by national necessity, had begun, but was far from complete
- registration and maintenance had provided a basic security for the men yet, because they were still not permanent employees and continued to rely on the 'free call' for their employment, their attitudes continued to reflect the casual era
- loyalty was given not to an employer, because the men did not have employers as such: instead they had the impersonal concept of the NDLB – the union continued to be their help in time of need, but above all it was 'every man for himself'.

As we have seen, the reverse side of the NDLB coin introduced administrative delay and indecision, and all of these factors caused the undermining of the piece-work system on which London's former prosperity depended. But by far the most serious aspect of deterioration was the general feeling of disaffection and malaise which marked the post-war era. The prevalent mood of the nation was that, having won World War II, we should now reap the rewards. Expectations increased immeasurably, as did the demand for more and more security. Perhaps the spirit of adventure and risk-taking had been squandered in a time of war, and peacetime brought with it yearnings for stability, a permanent job and a steady wage. All these expectations were not satisfied by the half-measures towards decasualisation which had been taken, and they were thwarted by the lack of any proper employer/employee relationship (in theory it was possible for a man to work for up to 11 employers in one week!) and by the continuance of the 'free-call' and a piece-work system which meant that for the same degree of effort a man could earn £10 in one week and £50 in the next. In times when increasing numbers of men were buying their own houses on mortgage, that was quite simply not good enough.

I have said that this was a twilight period in the docks. The old had gone and the new had yet to be born. In the halflight, London and many other ports paid the price, a price that in very many instances has not yet been redeemed.

It is significant that, in the eight years from 1930 to 1938, 285 man-days per 1,000 employees were lost in disputes in British ports. During the eight-year period from 1947 to 1955 the figure was 3,134, and between 1956 and 1964 it was 10,091. The figures speak for themselves. So far as London was concerned they resulted in a swelling assault on the port's reputation, and eventually on her trade. To say that the situation was exploited for left-wing political reasons is true, but no more than was to be expected in such a circumstance. It is also true that resistance to change among shipowners and employers, and by some of the men themselves, was a potent factor for the worse. But all in all it became increasingly evident that something was drastically wrong, and that only a swift advance to complete the already beginning process of decasualisation could hope to stem the tide.

4   The challenge of modernisation:
Devlin Stage One

The increasing time which ships had to spend in port, coupled with the increasingly heavy cost of running them and of the stevedoring operations, led the shipowners to introduce their first experiments in unitisation. This concept had been pioneered by the Port of London Authority and by Scruttons Ltd in the late 1940s, first in the East India and subsequently in the West India and Millwall docks; in the latter the experiment involved my own company. The idea was that if cargo could be prepacked at its place of origin – in the warehouse or factory – into larger units, these could be loaded into the ship more speedily, with less damage and requiring the work of fewer men. The shipowner would therefore enjoy substantial savings. The scheme was, above all, intended to cut down the number of days which a ship had to spend in port, days when she could not be earning money for her owners. This unitisation frequently took the form of palletisation: cases or cartons of cargo, usually fruit or tinned products, were pre-stowed on wooden pallets which could be transported by fork-lift trucks (at this time becoming readily available) to the ship. After the pallets had been lifted by the crane in the usual manner, another fork-lift truck conveyed them from the square of the ship's hatch into the far recesses of the hold. As a variation on this, the Fred Olsson Company introduced in Millwall Dock new vessels, *The Black Prince* and *The Black Watch,* which had doors in their sides to permit fork-lifts carrying pallets of Canary Island tomatoes to be driven straight from the quayside into the bowels of the vessels. The use of small fork-lift trucks for the easier handling of cargo on the quays was increasing at this time, and it became commonplace for work in alleyways or in the long 'run ins' in the holds to be facilitated by the use of transportable rollers, over which cartons or small packages of cargo could be rolled out speedily and with little effort.

All of these mechanical aids succeeded in improving turnaround and generally making life easier for the dock workers. What they did not do – certainly in the case of the private companies – was to reduce the numbers of men involved in the operations. This was to some extent due to the fact that, as long as a major part of the cargo had to be handled manually by traditional methods, it was unlikely that the mechanical aids could be used for more than a very few hours at a time. This allowed the trade unions to argue bitterly – as indeed they did – against any reduction in the numbers of men involved. As with all half-measures, these first attempts at modernisation failed in their principal objective, that of dramatically reducing costs. Also, because of the employers' constant argument with the unions over manning scales, they certainly did not help the cause of industrial relations either. What they did do was to provide a further pointer to the shape of things to come.

So far as our company was concerned, the fact that our ships were small ones – about 2,000 tons – precluded the use of much machinery, except for the 'work-saver' fork-lift appliances which we used from time to time to help the stevedores in the holds. However, it was concluded that the future lay in the provision of more and more machinery at greater and greater expense. This brought about a major change in the organisation and ownership of our family company. Ever since the end of the war we had, in addition to our Swedish business, done the work on vessels of Ellerman's Wilson Line that were trading with the Scandinavian countries. Ellerman's were then a very large and powerful ship-owning company, and had for many years owned a subsidiary, the Antwerp Steamship Company, a former shipping organisation which had survived as a stevedoring firm. But the war had deprived it of much of its management, and its former business had been given to us. We had no lack of management potential but, as a purely private family concern, our financial resources were limited. It was therefore natural that the two organisations should come together, and in due course L J Hovey Ltd was amalgamated with the Antwerp Steamship Company: the new company became known as Hovey Antwerp Ltd.

One of the first major changes of modernisation was to affect us. The concept of 'roll-on roll-off' operation – in which fully laden vehicles are driven onto the vessel and, after the sea voyage, driven off – had been developed in and after the war with the use of landing craft. These operations, based on Tilbury Docks, had been successful but inordinately expensive, as the employers continued to pay measurement piece-work rates for the relatively easy work involved in driving a lorry onto the ship and securing it. Moreover, the ships were handled under the provisions of the 'free call', so that the operations were modern in technology alone.

Another major initiative at Tilbury in the early 1960s was the establishment by the Port of London Authority of a specialised 'packaged timber' terminal. Timber was by then being prepacked into large units by mechanical means. Although based on earlier experience with self-contained 'shed crews', this was the first genuine 'terminal operation' in the Port of London. It was performed by a permanent team of PLA employees, who were paid a fixed wage with the option of additional over-time, irrespective of the amount of work they were actually required to do. This operation represented a clean break with every aspect of the casual system, and it set the scene for one of the next major developments which was to involve my own company.

Swedish Lloyd, with whom we had done business in Millwall Dock ever since their foundation half a century earlier, decided to replace their traditional cargo-and-passenger service from London to Gothenburg with a 'roll-on roll-off' service. For this enterprise they entered into a consortium with the Svea Company of Stockholm and with Ellerman's Wilson Line, with all three companies providing a vessel each for the service, which was known as the England Sweden Line. Its British terminal was to be at Tilbury. These were first-class passenger vessels, upholding the extremely high standards for which Swedish Lloyd had already gained a high reputation. The arrangements for the carriage of cargo were modern in the extreme. These were not 'roll-on roll-off' ships in the sense that the lorries bringing the cargo to the docks would themselves travel across the North Sea. The concept was that, in order to save space, the cargo was to be carried from its point of origin secured onto large frames measuring 20 ft by 8 ft or, failing that, to be assembled in such a way at Tilbury. The vehicles would depart, leaving some 200 units of cargo on plinths approximately two feet high. On the ship's arrival, all the dockers had to do was to use a hydraulic lifter to drive the load over a stern ramp into the ship, where a similar arrangement of plinths enabled the load to be deposited and secured while the hydraulic lifter was driven away. This cut the time for the discharge and loading of a cargo from a full week to a few hours.

The contract for this completely new form of stevedoring was put out to tender. Although our company had always been contractors to Swedish Lloyd, the odds were stacked against us. We had no experience whatsoever of anything like this form of work; our licence for the employment of dock workers extended only to Millwall and the Surrey Commercial Docks, where we employed Blue union men exclusively; above all, we had never worked at Tilbury or employed White union dockers, the only labour force there. Ranged against us were two of the largest and most efficient stevedoring companies in London, both of whom had some experience of this type of work.

We had, though, one advantage. Ellerman's Wilson Line, part-owners of Hovey Antwerp, were members of the ship-owning consortium England Sweden Line. I was personally determined to try to secure the contract for our company, and Ellerman's supported me (although I suspect they thought we had little chance of success). Myself, I was convinced that with an operation so new it was a positive asset never to have operated at Tilbury before, and particularly never to have worked with the White union. What was required was a complete break with the past, and who better to provide it, I thought, than a company that had not been associated with the practices of bygone years? In reply to the charge that we had never worked at Tilbury, our reply had to be that this was precisely why we were the company most likely to make the new concept succeed. New technology and new attitudes must march hand in hand.

I flew to Sweden to present our case to Swedish Lloyd. The first omens were not propitious. Gothenburg was shrouded, not unusually, in thick fog – hence its nickname 'Little London' – and the flight had to be diverted to Oslo, where we landed in driving snow. After a long and tiring train journey I arrived exhausted in my hotel in Kungsportsavenyn in the early hours of the next morning, and was able to snatch a few hours' sleep. Perhaps it was an advantage that I was able to make our case in Swedish – due to my father's foresight in making me learn the language. We were successful and were given the remarkable opportunity, for such a small company, of launching a new adventure for British Ports.

Swedish Lloyd had arranged with the Port of London Authority to lease a berth with adjacent quayspace at 26 Shed, Tilbury Docks. It was in the process of being equipped with a stern ramp for the loading of cargo, with first-class passenger embarkation facilities and with a large warehouse for the packing of the cargo into unit loads. Our company was, of course, concerned with the provision of labour. The first thing, since we had never operated at Tilbury, was to secure our employer's licence to do so. Since we already had the contract, and were more than able to meet the requirements of the Licensing Act (to offer full-time employment to about 40 men), the PLA – the Licensing Authority – had no hesitation in giving us the licence. The next thing was to secure the employees. I went to see Harry Freeman, the relevant official of the Transport and General Workers' Union at Tilbury Docks (subsequently to become a valued friend) and told him of the proposed operation and of our determination to give permanent employment at a high basic wage to a number of his members. I also made it clear that the uncertainties of piece-work had no place in this kind of operation: rate of work would be dictated not by muscle-power but by the speed of the machine, and a basic weekly wage would be paid for five days' work in every seven, with Saturday and Sunday regarded in principle as just like any of the other days. There would be some additional overtime, as required.

This was an entirely new concept at Tilbury, and Harry, together with Harry Battie, his branch chairman, must have wondered what had hit him. To their eternal credit they gave us the unstinting support without which we, as new boys to Tilbury, could not possibly have succeeded. (Dear Harry Battie, with his white cloth cap firmly and permanently planted on his head, was a tower of strength and a man of extreme authority among his fellows. He was an unfailing support until his untimely death some years later on the dance floor, where he loved to take his wife week by week).

I asked Harry Freeman whether he would tell me to which of his members I should offer employment. He was horrified, and asked me if I wanted him to be lynched by those that he did not nominate. He advised me to place an advertisement in the 'Pound', the local name for the NDLB muster point for the Tilbury men, asking for volunteers. There were some 2,000 men at Tilbury, and within about three days we had 300 applications for the 35 – 40 jobs on offer. We closed the lists forthwith, but were confronted with a task never before undertaken by a master stevedore: choosing which registered men to employ and which not to employ. I decided that each applicant must be interviewed separately and privately, and arranged with the PLA to lend me a small office at their Tilbury landing stage. There – with my longtime friend Fred Scott, who had been designated manager of the new terminal, to take notes – I interviewed all 300.

It was one of the most interesting exercises of my life, and was to condition many of my thoughts and actions over the next 20 years. As each man entered, I rose and asked him to be seated. Astonishment appeared on virtually every face. No employer had ever acted like this before. A few brief questions solicited why people were interested in the job. It was not the opportunity of high earnings – far greater amounts were available in the best piece-work gangs. What people wanted was a sense of belonging to a particular operation and employer, and above all the stability and security which permanency and a high basic wage on which they could rely week after week would give them. It was made clear that a lot of the men were involved in buying their own houses under mortgage and many of their creature comforts under hire purchase: our new concept was to them far more attractive than the vagaries and uncertainties of piece-work, whether as part of a regular or a 'floating' gang. On conclusion of the interview each man was thanked for his attendance with a handshake.

The next anecdote is apocryphal, but I am sure it is true. Most of the applicants were younger men, and on returning home they would have described the day's events to their father, or even grandfather, with the comment that 'The young guv'nor seems a decent sort of chap.' The reply would certainly have been, 'You watch him, I know what his father – or grandfather – used to do'!

In due course we selected our team. The difficulty was usually in deciding who *not* to take. There is, however, one unfortunate postscript. I have already referred to the fact that Irishmen dug and then worked in the London Docks. There was also a substantial Irish element at Tilbury. Fred Scott had secured the services of an excellent Irish ganger as foreman of the terminal and not unnaturally this man was anxious that some of his former colleagues should be included in our terminal team. I had not anticipated the result. For the only time in my life I was accused of religious discrimination. It transpired that, when the names of the team were made public, we had a disproportionate percentage of Roman Catholics.

I will add one postscript to the story of 26 Berth and the England Sweden Line. The chairman of Swedish Lloyd not unnaturally wished to use the occasion of the first visit of his fine new cargo/passenger liner, *The MV Saga,* to Tilbury to obtain maximum publicity. The ship arrived at 8am and was due to sail again at 5pm, having been fully discharged and loaded with prepacked units. A luncheon was held aboard, to which, in addition to the usual shippers and port dignitaries, representatives of the Swedish and the English press were invited. Our new team had had precisely one week's training in the use of the new machinery, but the job went without a hitch and the ship sailed to time. The Swedish journalists at first refused to believe that the men involved were indeed Tilbury dockers, and were convinced that the shipowners had imported 'men from Sweden' for the occasion. Such was the reputation – in this instance totally undeserved – which Britain's dockworkers had been given. I fervently hoped that this might be the beginning of putting the record straight.

At the beginning of the 1960s it was becoming increasingly obvious that the piecemeal introduction of modern-style operations such as the one described above was, if anything, exacerbating the general feeling of unease in the docks. The identification of the union leaders with management because of their association within the National Dock Labour Board had been one of the factors which had enabled unofficial leaders, particularly in the white union, to assume the *de facto* leadership of the rank-and-file in the Port of London. This was especially so in the giant Royal group of docks, on which most of the London shipowners depended, where Jack Dash emerged as perhaps the most effective unofficial leader of his day. Jack normally worked for Thames Stevedoring Company, a subsidiary of Lord Vestey's Blue Star Line. Although he was a constant thorn in their flesh and that of other major employers, he could never be accused of being a laggard when at work nor of inventing grievances. He was, however, a master of the art of magnifying the smallest of potential disagreements into a conflagration of the greatest magnitude. He was an expert on the platform, and a doughty debater at meetings. I remember only one occasion on which he was thwarted. After decasualisation, when Jack had been made a shop steward in the Royals, I had to attend as Chairman of the joint 'fire brigade' committee which both sides had established in order to deal swiftly with any incipient trouble. Jack, most unusually for him, was late, and the only remaining seat at the table was the one beside me. I was able to say: 'Come and sit next to me, Mr Dash.' He remained silent throughout the meeting, much to the consternation of the employers.

The relations between official and unofficial leaders can perhaps be illustrated by the story of a late-night visit to the BBC's Lime Grove studios in the late 1960s. At this time Jack was organising, with marked success, his series of half-day strikes in the Royals. So good was the organisation that nobody ever had more than about half an hour's foreknowledge of when the strikes would occur, and the Royals were in chaos as a result. The BBC asked Jack to make his case and I agreed to represent the employers provided that Peter Shea, the official union leader, was also present. (For an employer not to appear was always the kiss of death, as the BBC presenter would simply point to the empty chair and the case would go by default. It was equally damaging if an employer confronted an unofficial leader in the absence of his official counterpart.) After a short film of the Royal docks, the programme took the form of questions and answers, and by sheer good fortune I was able to give the final reply before the chairman closed the session. Jack's comment to the chairman – 'You're a fine one, giving the employer the last word like that' – indicated that the reply must have been effective! After the programme, all three of us accepted the BBC's invitation to a drink and were then given, as was the custom with guests on late-night programmes, chauffeured cars to take us home. As Jack and Peter both lived in Stepney, Peter suggested they should share a car. Jack's reply was: 'That would not be very suitable.' The tragedy of the London Docks was that by this time, although both official and unofficial leaders could and did talk to me, they could not talk to each other.

It was at the beginning of the 1960s that some of the more forward-looking shipowners began to see that the rather tentative measures so far taken in London to improve the men's security and safeguard their living standards had succeeded in doing little more than whet their appetites and turn them into easy victims for any agitator who, for political or other purposes, wished to bring chaos to the Port. The first wary efforts at technical innovation had been successful only up to a point, and were frustrated by the continuing malaise which was at least in part due to what remained of the casual system. The employers, for their part, were in the main deeply suspicious of further change, afraid no doubt of leaving the world which they had known for generations and venturing out into the unknown. On the other hand, the institution of 'fall-back guarantees' and the accelerating collapse of the piecework system was making the task of management more and more impossible: it had reached the point where talented managers, far from dictating the course of events, spent almost the whole of their working day reacting to events and 'fighting fires' that should never have broken out.

The continuing drain of Britain's – and particularly London's – trade to the Continent meant that this was affecting the nation as a whole – an effect compounded by the fact that a strike in London or Liverpool was likely to cause a run on the pound. The whiff of even more radical technical innovation was in the air. Clearly it was a time of challenge and a time for change.

The time and the man came together in the person of a younger shipowner, David Lloyd. As a director of Ellerman Lines, he had the ear of the senior shipowners. David was convinced that the way forward lay in the removal of the last vestiges of the casual system through the attachment of all registered dockworkers to permanent employers. This clearly spelt the end of the smaller stevedoring firms, which employed labour only on a sporadic basis and which had anyway tended to be the less responsible members of the fraternity.

David Lloyd, who by now had succeeded Andrew (subsequently Sir Andrew) Crichton of P&O as chairman of the London Shipowners' Dock Labour Committee, had the support of the majority of his senior colleagues. He set up a committee (on which I later served), to consider how to achieve decasualisation. After thorough investigation and very much argument, it produced differing proposals.

The first was to insist that only employers who could employ their labour on a full-time basis should continue in business. The second was that an 'employing consortium', including all the employers, should be set up to engage all the men permanently; this consortium would allocate the men on a daily basis to those employers who actually needed them.

The second of these proposals represented, in essence, the views of those master stevedores who wished to hang on to any possible advantages of the casual system while at the same time accepting the principle of decasualisation. The first – which was far more radical – was designed to ensure that in future every man would have his own permanent employer; thus, for the first time, there was the possibility of building up a proper relationship between the employers and the vast majority of their employees. This more radical proposal would, however, involve a reduction in the number of employers in the Port of London from 50 or so to a maximum of 10 or 11. It was an interesting fact that, with one major exception and one borderline case, all these 'spared' employers were either fully owned or very closely identified with major shipowners. Blue Star Line had long owned the Thames Stevedoring Company. Glen Line, Union Castle and Furness Withy had set up a new consortium in the Royal Docks called Southern Stevedores. Elder Dempsters had established the Metropolitan Stevedoring Company at Tilbury and Furness Withy had their own stevedoring companies in the Surrey Commercial Docks and at Millwall. Our own company, Hovey Antwerp (which, as I have said, was better placed than most because of the regular nature of its work), was closely bound to the Ellerman Group.

I regarded it – and still regard it – as entirely appropriate that the shipowners, for whom after all the ports exist, should themselves accept responsibility for the dockworkers upon whose labours they so often depend for the prosperity of their businesses. But this was not the traditional view. It had been for generations the habit of British shipowners to distance themselves from the dockworkers by picking and choosing among the stevedoring contractors. Because of the competition, prices were low. Most importantly, the shipowners could keep out of the 'dirty end of the business' – which, because of this policy, they very often did not fully understand. Above all, the fact that they did not employ the men directly meant that, as soon as a ship had sailed, the shipowners had absolutely no responsibility for the men until their ship returned. It is little wonder that lack of responsibility in one direction bred an equal irresponsibility in return.

In the event, David Lloyd's bold initiative was overtaken by events. Before action could be taken on either of the proposals, the situation in the docks had become so much worse that the government of the day, under Harold Macmillan, decided to intervene. They commissioned the High Court judge, Lord Devlin, to report on the steps which needed to be taken to achieve full decasualisation of labour, and to secure the way forward in the industry.

Lord Devlin was assisted in his enquiry by Jack Scamp and Hugh Clegg. I recall being asked by Hugh Clegg to give my views. He held court for this purpose in the superintendent's office in the Royal Docks. The subject on which he chose to question me was that of employer/employee relationships. In general, because of the casual nature of the industry, these were largely non-existent, but our company, a small one with many 'regulars', was an exception. I still recall the disbelief on Clegg's face (he was an eminent academic and I imagine felt himself confronted with a wayward pupil trying to pull the wool over his eyes) when I told him a true story dating from the time when I had worked at Millwall and lived in Kensington. It was my habit to take the bus from Pier Head to Mile End Station, and then the tube to the West End. Often work would end at about 8pm and, true to naval tradition, I would wait until the last minute before leaving the ship for the bus-stop. It was no infrequent thing, as I queued, for a car laden with dockers to sweep out of the dock gate and screech to a halt by me.

'Where do you want to go, Guv?'

'Mile End.'

'Hop in.'

I suppose that was an example of the better kind of employer/employee relationship, but I still wonder what Clegg reported to Devlin!

The Devlin Report was certainly the most important document to affect the docks since the Shaw Report of 1922. Devlin, with incisive judicial clarity, did not fudge the issue. The casual system, which he believed lay at the root of all the problems because it bred irresponsibility and sloppy attitudes, had to go – lock, stock and barrel. The first part of his report (Devlin Stage One) prescribed the precise method of achieving the attachment of every man to a regular employer. The second part (Devlin Stage Two) emphasised the necessity to introduce further reforms – notably to the payments system – to eliminate anything associated with the casual attitudes of the past. The employers were in particular castigated for their failure to bring about change and for their failure to provide proper amenities for the men.

In so far as Stage One was concerned, there is little doubt that Devlin was privy to the two proposals produced by David Lloyd's committee. The proposed consortium would have provided a platform for the indefinite continuance of casual attitudes, and so Devlin had no hesitation in proposing the root-and-branch solution whereby all the dockers were permanently attached to a much smaller number of employers.

There were many last-minute efforts by minor employers to combine forces in the hope of survival, but these were of little avail. The successful applicants for the new employers' licences were the large concerns – nearly all shipowner-backed – which were able to command substantial business, and to a few small specialist companies which had a virtual monopoly in certain regular trades. (Our firm was one of these specialist companies.)

Mention should be made of the single major exception to the involvement of the shipowners with the new licensed employers. The largest private stevedoring company, Scruttons, had some years earlier merged its business with the second largest, T. F. Maltby, to form Scruttons Maltby. The size of this business, second only to that of Port of London Authority itself, and its well deserved reputation for efficiency, enabled it to continue without the support of any particular shipowning group of the many (including P&O) that were numbered among its clients. Its efficiency, however, may have been wedded to piecework and some of the concepts of casualism more than most of its rivals.

The recommendations of the Devlin Report – which included also the setting up of national and local modernisation committees in the ports to oversee the steps to be taken under Stage Two – were given the force of law by the Docks and Harbours Act of 1966 and the dock workers (Regulation of Employment)(Amendment) Order of 1967. On 18 September 1967, complete decasualisation of the dock labour force was at last achieved.

I remember arriving at Millwall in time for the start of the first day's work under the new arrangements. I addressed our 300-odd permanent employees from the top of a fork-lift truck. The message was simple: from now on, like it or not, we are in the same boat together. If we do well, so will you. If you fail us, we shall go under. The future can be a bright one, but it is in all of our hands.

The men in our company went to work with a will and, until factors outside our control intervened, our experience of decasualisation was a happy one.

In addition to the creation of the national and local modernisation committees, David Lloyd and his shipowner colleagues had decided to reorganise the employers' side of the industrial machinery in London. Hitherto the shipowners had always themselves played a leading role, a very senior shipowner being chairman of the 'London Ten' (the policy-making committee of the London employers) and another (now David Lloyd) being chairman of the London Shipowners' Dock Labour Committee, which negotiated directly with the trade unions in the docks. Lloyd took the undoubtedly correct view that, with the establishment of the new and generally shipowner-controlled employers, it was now the responsibility of these employers to take charge of their side of the industry. Accordingly, the shipowners set up an employers' organisation – the London Ocean Trades Employers' Association. All of the licensed employers became members (apart from PLA, which had its own separate negotiating machinery in the enclosed docks). John Kiernan, from Furness Withy, became chairman of this body, and I became vice-chairman (later I succeeded John as chairman). This meant that both of us also had to take the chair from time to time as joint-chairman of the Ocean Trades Group Joint Committee which, together with the PLA Group Joint Committee, constituted the main negotiating body for the enclosed docks. In parallel, John and I were appointed to the Local Modernisation Committee for London, of which I also subsequently became joint chairman.

One of the first tasks now confronting the employers was the appointment (specifically recommended by Devlin) of official shop stewards; before this, only the PLA had had the experience of shop stewards. It was hoped that this move would effectively undermine the activities of the unofficial activists who had been such a thorn in the flesh to both the employers and the official trade-union leaders.

However, the planners had reckoned without the obtuseness of human nature. So far as our own company was concerned, the appointment of shop stewards was virtually a total success. Our formula was that a shop steward's function was to 'oil the works' so that the company did as well as possible; it would then be for the company to ensure that the men did equally well in every respect. The experience of some of the other companies was very different. Scruttons Maltby, in particular, employed a large labour force (some 2,000 men in the Royal Docks alone), and it was with their company that Jack Dash and his fellow unofficials had wrought the most havoc. However, these men were the leaders whom the dockers in the Royals had chosen to follow; it should perhaps have been no surprise when the workers elected them *en bloc* as their official shop stewards. Not unnaturally, the employers were dismayed, and it needed a quite extraordinary degree of imagination to think that these same individuals, who for years had been dedicated to causing friction, would overnight, simply by virtue of having put on another cap, accept my formula of 'oiling the works', for the benefit of all.

Worst of all, if the shop-steward system was to succeed – and it was a lynchpin of the modernisation scheme – then adequate facilities and help, sometimes paid time-off included, had to be given by the employers. One of the most difficult and unpleasant tasks I ever had was to persuade my friend Robin Hampson, the highly dedicated and forward-looking managing director of Scruttons Maltby that he had no alternative to paying Jack Dash and his colleagues for disrupting his company if they chose to do so.

It was a difficult situation, not helped by the fact that decasualisation actually sparked off a major strike in the Liverpool and London docks (in the latter port it was largely confined to the Royals). At issue was the amount of the daily guarantee that would be paid to dockers at all times, whether work was available or not. The amount of the guarantee was the subject of last-minute argument between the two sides, and the government eventually decided on an arbitrary figure. It was this to which the men in London and Liverpool objected: they felt that more might have been extorted by more aggressive union bargaining. The strike in both ports was led by the former unofficials – now, of course, shop stewards – a fact which hardly inspired confidence in the new system or in those dedicated to making it work.

Part and parcel of Devlin Stage One was meant to be the removal of all time-wasting or 'restrictive' practices, but it quickly became apparent that many of these had been not only spawned by but also entrenched in the piecework system. The problem was that over the previous two decades, the employers, in trying to make the system work, had watered it down until it no longer served as an incentive to hard work; rather, it had become an excuse for delay and a seedbed for argument. Men working on the most rewarding piecework commodities might not even be prepared to work at all until guaranteed that large sums would be added to their piecework earnings at the end of the day. It was soon evident, particularly in the larger companies, that many of these practices were not going to be removed overnight simply by changing the status of the dock-worker and the nature of his attachment to a permanent employer. Wisely, the National Modernisation Committee recognised that in many ports, especially the larger ones, only a root-and-branch change in the payment system – with far greater emphasis on stability of earnings and far less, if any, on piecework – would enable the problems to be dealt with effectively.

Perhaps the most tangible of Devlin's recommendations concerned his appalledness at the lack of ordinary human amenities in dockland. Toilet facilities were of the most primitive kind (frequently nineteenth-century relics) and canteens were virtually nonexistent. The Harbours Act of 1966 laid on the National Dock Labour Board the duty of providing modern industrial canteens and toilet blocks throughout the docks. The Port of London Authority played a central role in drawing up the plans for London, and one of the more improbable tasks of the amenities committee on which I sat was to visit the different canteens with a trade-union colleague to sample the various wares and convince the men – in some areas they needed no convincing – that there was nothing sinister in the employers' provision of these facilities and that they should indeed use them.

Not unnaturally, there was considerable political interest in the programme of modernisation for the docks. A Labour government was in power at the time, and there is no doubt that its support for trade-union policy was a potent factor in driving the programme forward.

The political event that I recall most clearly, however, was a visit to the docks by Margaret Thatcher (then newly appointed as Shadow Minister of Transport) and Michael Heseltine. I imagine she had asked for a briefing on the London dock situation, then always in the news. Dudley

Perkins, the PLA's Director General, headed the escorting party of which I was a part. I walked down the north side of the Victoria Dock side-by-side with the woman who would later become Prime Minister. We passed a Blue Star ship where men were handling carcasses of meat destined for the cold-store installation. As we came abreast of them one of the dockers shouted out: 'I suppose you're the Tories' Barbara Castle.' Without a moment's hesitation she shouted back: 'Yes, that's right, but 20 years younger!'

We all lunched aboard Shaw Savill's *Gothic* in the Royal Docks, and then drove to Tilbury to see the PLA's new dock developments there. Afterwards we visited the Hovey Antwerp operation at 26 Berth. Thatcher asked if she might meet some of the men. Fortunately it was tea break, and about 50 dockers, including some very voluble shop stewards, were in our canteen. I provided both our visitors with large mugs of tea and thrust them into the melee. They were soon engaged in animated discussion, particularly with the stewards, and I thought it wise to keep in the background. I heard afterwards that, although they did not agree with everything she said, she went down very well. Michael Heseltine fared less successfully, being associated rather too blatantly, as far as the dockers were concerned, with the 'old school tie'.

The three years between Devlin Stage One and Devlin Stage Two were increasingly difficult and frustrating. It was not that any major disagreement existed regarding decasualisation. Shipowners, employers, trade unions and the dockers themselves all accepted it as the way forward – most because, after reflection, they believed in it, and others because they felt it was inevitable. The difficulties stemmed primarily from the continuance of the attitudes born out of the casual system, attitudes enhanced by the continuation of piecework and all of the opportunities for argument that surrounded it.

At this critical juncture another sinister element entered the field. The number of registered dockworkers in London had peaked during the 1950s. In the early 1960s any reduction in the register had been relatively easily coped with by natural wastage. Now the pace of loss accelerated, and the results for the industry were traumatic.

For many decades the dockworkers had striven for the essential securities – job and earnings – which most manual workers had long taken for granted. It was only in 1967 that the dockers finally achieved security of tenure and a high basic wage.

But no sooner had security of employment been achieved than the employment itself was threatened. The causes of the decline in London's trade were manifold. Some were outside the control of both employers and men, but in other cases the industry had only itself to blame. Many days were lost by strike and argument in London and the other large ports, and there was a general air of uncertainty surrounding their use. These factors, coupled with increasing expense, meant that many other smaller ports, particularly those on the east and south coasts of England, were enabled to grow and prosper. Many of them, such as Kings Lynn, Lowestoft and Ipswich, had an ancient history: now they were able to build and expand their traditional business, in the certainty of having a captive market among the shipowners. This coincided with the shipowners' willingness to modernise, so that many firms, specialising in ro-ro or in the handling of packaged goods, were established up and down the east coast.

The most notable example of such development was Felixstowe. It had been virtually unknown as a port before World War II, when it was a base for flying boats. After that war, the derelict harbour was acquired by an East Anglian miller, Gordon Parker, as part of a larger parcel of land. He saw the possibilities that might lie ahead. Despite a major setback caused by the severe east-coast floods of the 1950s, the development of Felixstowe as an exclusively modern port continued. From the outset only nonconventional cargo – palletised, packaged, or in some way unitised – was handled. Ships failing to meet this criterion were rejected and obliged to use traditional ports such as London. The inbuilt advantage this policy gave to Felixstowe was regarded by many as unfair. Piecework was never entertained. From the beginning the men – of good East Anglian farming stock – came in from the fields and exchanged their tractors for dock machinery (subsequently for straddle carriers). Their wives came, too, to help in the canteen. A family atmosphere was created, and to some extent it still remains. The men enjoyed good stable wages. Union influences were not strong and, where they existed, were at local rather than national level. In short, none of the history which had conditioned the workers in the major ports, and none of the resulting trauma, affected Felixstowe. No wonder the beleaguered shipowners, with the freedom to send their vessels where they chose, looked on Felixstowe as a veritable paradise.

Another major reason for London's decline, again stemming from its own failures, was the loss of trans-shipment cargoes to Rotterdam and Antwerp. In the days of Empire, great quantities of continental cargo were handled in London. Ships from all parts of the globe had discharged in the Thames, offloading those parts of their cargoes that were consigned to continental Europe onto coasting or smaller craft, which then took them across the Channel to their destinations. Now, because of the inordinate delays incurred in London, the situation went into reverse. Ships instead went to Rotterdam and Antwerp, where they could work unhindered, and their London cargoes were ferried to a number of English ports as and when required. London dockers were thereby deprived of thousands of jobs. Unhappily, this situation still continues. In spite of the advent of containers, the position has never been fully recovered.

Why was the industry blind to the possible extent of this self-inflicted injury? From 1965, when I was virtually seconded from my family company by the shipowners to work on the modernisation of the industry, I saw at first hand some of the attitudes which prevailed. Week after week I or my trade-union opposite number would preside at a meeting of the Ocean Trades Group Joint Committee, usually to receive reports from the Piecework Sub-Committee concerning innumerable disputes that were causing problems and often stoppages in the docks. Week after week we would point out that more and more shipping lines were deserting London in favour of the east coast or the Continent. The mens' representatives knew the truth, but were reluctant to face it. But the dockers themselves (although their numbers were reducing year by year through natural wastage and later by voluntary severance) were, as a result of manipulation of the piecework system and the weakness of the employers, who were determined at almost any cost to prevent it from breaking down entirely, earning more and more. Under these circumstances, and in the absence of a strong lead from their Trade Union, perhaps it was over optimistic to expect them to know how increasingly weak their position was becoming. In the end, the bubble burst. Afterwards the inevitable accusations of mismanagement and lack of confidence in the trade unions made matters go from bad to worse.

There are many stories about the meetings of the Ocean Trades Group Joint Committee and the London Modernisation Committee. My deputy on both was a very fine and intensely loyal retired Lieutenant-Commander from the Royal Navy. He had been trained in the discipline of the Senior Service, and was inclined to rule by the book. On one occasion, after a short holiday, I returned to find that a problem (as far as I can recall, a trivial one) had arisen in the Royal Group of docks, and that my deputy had quite properly called an emergency meeting of the Group Joint Committee. I asked the joint secretary – who was 'neutral' in these matters – to brief me and then instructed the employers' representatives, of which there were seven or eight, to remain silent until I called on them from the chair. When the union representatives entered and sat opposite the employers at our long narrow table at Mansell Street, with me and the joint secretary sitting rather forlornly at the head, they were at full strength – about a dozen. This was an ominous sign.

On this occasion my friend Bill Munday led for the unions. He was a giant of a man, very broad and thick in the neck, and was raring to go. Fortunately Bill always wore his heart on his sleeve: he could not have been deceitful if he had tried. On the other hand, his ire (when aroused) and his vocabulary were legendary. As soon as Bill was seated on my left, and before he had time to explode, I asked him politely and quietly what the trouble was. Bill tried hard to be calm, but I could see the blood rising in his neck as his natural ebullience overflowed in venom against the luckless employer. I pushed my chair back slightly, waited for Bill to run out of steam, and held my peace. The employers, on instruction, remained silent, although they would have loved to reply in kind. After a decent interval I turned to Les Newman, the leader of the blue union, on Bill's left, and asked him quietly for his views. And so on down the line, all 12 of them. The venom evaporated as we went on, and at the end of it they were exhausted: now that it had all been said, it was clear that it amounted to very little. It was then safe to let the employers reply. Had they done so earlier, the meeting would certainly have broken up in a furore, the problem been made worse, and threats of strike action likely.

Patience was certainly a virtue when dealing with the trade unions.

Knowledge of the men and their attitudes was perhaps even more important. Nothing was more likely to fan the flames of discontent than for an employer – and worst of all a chairman – not to know what he or she was talking about. The other thing one always had to remember and respect was that each trade-union leader, in presenting the case for the dockers, was speaking not only to the employers: indeed, he was speaking not so much to the employers as to his own colleagues and for the record. Every spoken word was carefully minuted, and agreement to the minutes of the last meeting was often the most difficult thing to achieve. In the case of the blue union, particularly, the performances of elected officials at these meetings were carefully scrutinized. A poor showing could cost them their jobs.

There were 'characters' on both sides in these meetings. Charlie Stebbings, a one-time leader of the blues, suffered from what one might normally think to be a disadvantage: he had to wear a deaf-aid. It was, however, electrically controlled. Whenever Charlie was being worsted in argument, he merely switched off his aid. Now that he was as deaf as a post, the argument was over.

The shipowners and employers were not above such ruses. At the end of our long conference table at the Mansell Street headquarters of LOTEA there was, hidden under the table by my place, a bell-push. This communicated with the secretary's office. If an especially contentious meeting was in prospect we would invariably instruct our loyal staff of lady secretaries to have tea perpetually 'at the ready'. Whenever I arrived at a point during a meeting when a walkout was imminent or a disaster threatened, I would ring the bell. The girls would enter like an army of avenging angels bearing their tea-trays laden with cups, and the consequent clatter of crockery as tea was passed around the room would effectively bring all conversation to an end. The respite often cooled tempers and, as well, allowed me a few precious moments of reflection that saved the day and prevented unpleasant and costly consequences.

On one occasion when I was serving as Chairman of the London Modernisation Committee my patience was almost at an end. The 'tea-ploy' had been tried and had failed. Bill Munday had reached the end of his tether, and he got up to walk out of the meeting – followed, with a greater or lesser degree of willingness, by his cohorts. The issue was a grave one, and could well have set back the progress of modernisation indefinitely. I said a silent prayer, and to my surprise Bill, with his hand on the door knob, suddenly turned round and walked back to his seat, indicating that he had had 'second thoughts'. His colleagues dutifully followed him, and somehow or other we got to the end of the meeting without disaster. The power of prayer!

The stories about such meetings are legion, and each of the participants will have his own particular memories. Suffice it to say that all of the people involved were trying to prop up a system which was collapsing because of its own ineptitude. This state of affairs could not in any event have long continued, but the next stage in events was precipitated by a new and potent factor which now, for the first time in earnest, had to be taken into account.

For some years the British shipowners had been following with interest and some anxiety the activities of the US inland-haulage contractor Malcolm Maclean. Maclean was also in the business of conveying sugar from Hawaii to the eastern seaboard of the United States. He conceived the notion that many man-hours of handling could be saved if the cargo was stowed at its point of origin in a large cargo container which could be used during both the sea voyage and the inland haul. The idea – simplicity itself in its conception – was to create a revolution in the shipping of cargoes greater than any since sail gave way to steam in the second half of the nineteenth century. Maclean's notion soon spread within the United States, and it was not long before its potential for international trade was recognised by the major trading nations of the world.

British shipowners were, from the start, at the forefront of the investigations into this new system. In the days when much of the deep-sea traffic on the main trade routes of the world was still carried in British vessels, the shipowners were particularly vulnerable to competition from container vessels, whose far greater speed of turnaround, greater carrying capacity and many other factors were likely to make them much more economic than the conventional cargo liners. The British shipowners therefore decided, in principle, to embark on containerisation. They were spurred on by the inordinate delays in turning round conventional vessels, particularly at British and Australian ports, and by the fact that a major rebuilding programme of conventional cargo liners was required if they were to continue as they had in the past.

It was planned that one giant container vessel would carry the same cargo as 8 – 10 conventional liners, and that a quantity of cargo that had previously taken three weeks of 10-hour days to load and discharge in the Royal Group would now be handled in 36 hours, working round the clock, at a purpose-built container terminal. As a bonus, the number of dockers required to load and discharge such a vessel would, it was thought, be one tenth of those employed on a conventional cargo liner. The arguments were convincing, and a study team was sent to the United States to report back to a group of senior British shipowners, including the chairmen of P&O, Cunard, British & Commonwealth (Union Castle), Furness Withy, Ellermans and Blue Star.

It was decided to go ahead with a pilot scheme in the Europe Australia Trade, which had been traditionally dominated by P&O, Port Line, Shaw Savill and Ellermans. The investments required were such that it became apparent from the outset that few, if any, individual shipowners could hope to 'go it alone'. The British shipowners preserved an element of the competition so dear to them by dividing into two camps: P&O, Blue Funnel of Liverpool (Ocean), British & Commonwealth and Furness Withy formed Overseas Containers Ltd to look after their container interests in the various trades, while Port Line, Shaw Savill, Blue Star, Ellermans, the New Zealand Shipping Company and Ben Line formed a rival consortium called Associated Container Transportation Ltd on a much looser basis under which considerable independence remained with the individual operators.

Apart from the hardware of ships and containers, two of the principal requirements were terminal facilities and a labour force prepared to operate them. The consortia decided that the first trade to be containerised should be that between northern Europe and Australasia, a trade that had traditionally been dominated by British Shipowners. Tilbury was chosen to be the terminal port for the United Kingdom. The Port of London Authority, under their Director General, Dudley Perkins, had as far back as 1962 made a vital and far-reaching decision to build a new dock to the southeast of the existing Tilbury Docks. This was to be large and deep enough to accommodate the contemplated container vessels as well as other ships bearing unitised cargo such as timber, paper and wood pulp. The new dock started operating in 1967, the year of Devlin Stage One. Its existence was to be the last major factor in the industrial drama surrounding the negotiation of Devlin Stage Two.

Before the tale of this drama is told (see Chapter 5) it might be well to take a good look at the players. Division was, as usual, rife. The shipowners were divided, the employers were divided, the trade unions were divided and the men were often divided.

Two factors alone provided some unity. Lord Devlin was sure of the principles of what should be done. Anything which smacked of casualism and casual attitudes must go. His was a voice of reason and, at least in principle, all the parties accepted it. But Lord Devlin did not lay down a time-scale or attempt to indicate how the reforms necessary to remove casual attitudes (particularly the reforms to the payments system) should be carried out. It was here that the differing interests immediately showed themselves. The shipowners were split between those whose principal concern was to launch their container investment at Tilbury as soon as possible, and those who were equally if not more keen to see their conventional ships working well and at a profit. The employers were divided between those who believed that the piecework system had served its useful purpose (at any rate it was wholly inappropriate for container work, in which the rate of production is controlled not by the physical effort of the man but even more by the speed of the machine) and that any attempt to preserve a 'bonus' element of any kind would merely preserve casual attitudes, and those who felt that a move towards a high upstanding wage, payable at all times, would result in a disastrous loss of production on the conventional ships. The unions were split in a more fundamental way, along inter-union lines between the whites (TGWU) and blues (NASD). The NASD had come to being in London to protect the interests of the 'craftsmen', the stevedores who loaded the vessels. They performed ship work in all the London docks except Tilbury, and dominated the Surrey Commercial Dock. In the post-war period, however, they had started to spread their wings, particularly in the east-coast port of Hull, where they were in due course accused of poaching members from the rival TGWU. This was prohibited under the terms of the Bridlington Agreement. As a result, the stevedores' union was disaffiliated from the TUC and lost its seat on the National Joint Council for the Port Transport Industry. Not unnaturally, this situation created considerable bitterness between the two unions, particularly at the higher levels: for example, the NASD was not allowed to be represented on the Port of London Executive Committee, the senior joint decision-making committee in the Port of London. The NASD was, nevertheless, represented at dock level through the Ocean Trades Group Joint Committee (and its junior committees). The result of this situation, so far as employers were concerned, was that the port became yet more ungovernable. In many situations – particularly in the ever-troublesome Royal Docks – TGWU and NASD members worked alongside one another continuously without problem. But, when difficulties arose, it was often sufficient for a TGWU leader to accept a solution for his NASD counterpart to disagree with it. The employer had, therefore, the difficult task of finding common ground between the two unions before any progress could be made.

Lord Devlin had the insight to realise that any realistic programme of modernisation would be stillborn unless an end were put to this feud. In his report he recommended strongly that the NASD's membership of the National Joint Council, and with it their access to the negotiating machinery of the industry, should be restored to them. He also ensured that they should receive due representation on the new National Modernisation Committee and on local modernisation committees.

But, although the rivalry between the unions diminished and a sincere effort was made to solve the Hull problem, major contentions remained, and these continued to plague the employers during the run-up to Devlin Stage Two. In particular, the TGWU became increasingly involved with container developments at Tilbury, from which the NASD members were excluded. The NASD, for their part, became increasingly worried about their dominant position in the Surrey Commercial Docks, because the packaging of timber in vessels was changing the nature of the business and the larger vessels which carried it were increasingly berthing at Tilbury rather than at the Surrey Commercial Docks. The PLA had built modern timber-handling facilities at Tilbury, which was a TGWU preserve. All this tended, not unnaturally, to put the NASD on the defensive. In the arguments that followed, the TGWU tended by and large to support those who sought to break new ground in facing the future while the NASD generally sided with those who sought to hang on to what remained of the past.

So far as the men themselves were concerned, the vast majority who had suffered the most from the old systems undoubtedly welcomed change – in particular, anything which added to job security and

Sailing barges locking out of the Surrey
commercial docks in the 1930s. (*Courtesy PLA
Collection/Museum in Docklands Project*)

Wet salted hides were imported raw from the tanner's trade and not infrequently became infested with maggots during the voyage. (*Courtesy PLA Collection/Museum in Docklands Project*)

Pre-war motor cars being lifted in nets and hoisted aboard with spreaders to minimise damage. Today they would be driven aboard purpose-built vessels. (*Courtesy PLA Collection/ Museum in Docklands Project*)

A typical post-war scene on a loading berth in the Royal Docks. General cargo is being stowed in the tween-deck and two railway coaches for Rhodesia have been placed on deck. (*Courtesy PLA Collection/Museum in Docklands Project*)

Below: The interior of one of the post-war PLA warehouses, showing the vast assortment of general cargo shipped through them. (*Courtesy PLA Collection/Museum in Docklands project*)
Right: Over this plank the lumpers would carry the heavy planks on their shoulders, one or two at a time, sometimes at a walk, sometimes at a run, and deposit them on the ever-rising stack. (*Courtesy PLA Collection/Museum in Docklands Project*)

Presiding like a mother hen over her chicks was the Swedish Lloyd passenger steamer, lying at her berth regularly from Monday to Saturday. (*Courtesy PLA Collection/Museum in Docklands Project*)

Left: I shall always remember walking down the north side of the Victoria Dock side-by-side with the future Prime Minister. **Below**: Margaret Thatcher in conversation with Harry Battie in the canteen at 26 Berth, Tilbury Docks.

Below: An aerial view of the Royal group of docks in 1946, immediately after the Second World War, when activity was at its height. (*Courtesy PLA Collection/Museum in Docklands Project*) **Left**: The author at the time of Devlin Stage Two, shortly before his appointment to Southampton. (*Peter Coppock*)

stability of wages. However, for those in the 'blue-eyed' gangs, and this category included most of the NASD men, the situation was different. Although they would gain job security, their guaranteed weekly wage packet would inevitably be smaller than the average take-home pay to which they had become accustomed. The more that they and their employers had connived at 'milking' the failing piecework system during previous years, the greater the discrepancy.

The final piece of the jigsaw puzzle fell into place on 3 January 1968. The TGWU, quite justifiably, was worried that the piecemeal introduction of local agreements on modern methods of handling (three or four had already been approved at Tilbury, including that for the England-Sweden Line) might make it more difficult for that vast majority of their members who were not employed under these new agreements to improve their own terms and conditions. The union therefore imposed a ban on the operation of OCL's new container berth at Tilbury and made it clear that, although not opposed to the introduction of containerisation, it would not allow the shipowners to use a facility which was a vital part of their massive new investment or permit a few of its members to benefit from the improved wages and conditions of employment until such time as it considered that sufficient progress had been made towards safeguarding its other members under the provisions of Devlin Stage Two.

The union could not have chosen a more effective lever. The Port of London Authority, who were to provide the labour for the new container terminal and had already negotiated an agreement with their local TGWU officials to do so, were frustrated by the ban. The shipowners had to suffer the loss and ignominy of sending their first container vessels to continental ports, to and from which the British cargo had to be transported at great expense. The more frustrated they became, the more the union realised the strength of its position and the tougher became its negotiating position on Stage Two, which alone could unlock the key to the container terminal.

Thus was the scene set for what were to be my last three years in the Port of London, from the introduction of Devlin Stage One in September 1967 to that of Devlin Stage Two in September 1970. They were years of intense activity. Meetings of the London Ocean Trades Employers' Association, the Ocean Shipowners' Group Joint Committee or the

London Modernisation Committee were held, on average, at the rate of five per week: frequently two were held on the one day. Added to these were reference-back meetings with the shipowners and visits to the Department of Employment either to seek advice or to be given it!

Initially I was vice-chairman – subsequently I became chairman – of all three committees, and I can testify that it was a full-time business. I recall attending a dinner-party at which our doctor was also present. I chatted about how, on several evenings a week, I would finish meetings with the trade unions at say 6.00pm; then at least two hours would be spent ringing round the various newspaper correspondents in an attempt to ensure that they received a factual and hopefully positive account of the day's doings. Failure to take this precaution unfailingly meant speculative articles and sometimes hostile banner headlines. When this exercise was complete, I would walk to Bank station en route for Waterloo and hence my home in Sunningdale. The quickest way lay down Leadenhall Street and Cornhill: it was noticeable that the only lighted windows of the shipping offices were those of the respective chairmen. On boarding at Waterloo I invariably fell asleep, waking up as the train reached Sunningdale. I suggested to our doctor that I was becoming a 'sleep-addict'. His reply was that, if I could 'cut off' after my standard day's programme, I had much to be grateful for. In retrospect, it was by such expedients that myself and others learned to survive the pressures.

5 The challenge of modernisation: Devlin Stage Two

Lord Devlin had correctly identified that the key to the final abolition of casual attitudes lay in the reform of the payments system. I had long been convinced, both by experience of the modern forms of cargo handling and by the extent to which the old systems had deteriorated (and were still continuing to do so) that a radical solution was the only course open to the employers. I therefore found it much easier to make common cause with those shipowners, employers and trade unionists who favoured a complete break with the past than with the very substantial body, particularly among my fellow master stevedores, who sought to delay as long as possible any more change than was absolutely necessary to meet Devlin's criteria, and who hankered – perhaps unconsciously – to maintain as much as they could of the old system. I was convinced that any exercise that merely involved cutting away the extremities and leaving the main body of the system unchanged would merely allow the cancerous tissues to grow again, and delay the inevitable major surgery. I remember confiding to George Cattell, who had been appointed by the government to be Chairman of the National Modernisation Committee, that 'the patient is so sick that we must lay him out on the slab, and only resuscitate him when he can no longer recollect the past'. That was a forlorn hope, but it perhaps indicates the serious state of affairs that existed as we approached Devlin Stage Two.

My authority, as Chairman of the London Ocean Trades Employers' Association (LOTEA), sprang from the shipowners, who had asked me to be first vice-chairman and subsequently (on John Kiernan's promotion to lead the London Executive Committee) chairman. The shipowners were not themselves members of LOTEA, but either directly or indirectly were able to exert authority over virtually all of the employers.

With the Tilbury ban gnawing at their purse-strings, the shipowners were quick to realise how important were the issues at stake and why they should exert their own influence on affairs. They consequently formed a high-powered Committee of Senior Liner Shipowners. This came to be affectionately known as the 'Grannies' Committee'. Presided over with avuncular rectitude and purpose by Sir Donald Anderson, it included in its membership Sir Nicholas Cayzer, Sir Basil Smallpiece, Ronald Vestey, Sir Andrew Crichton and Dennis Martin-Jenkins. During these critical times these gentlemen met on several occasions. My friend Walter Lewis, of Furness Withy, who was the shipowners' official 'adviser' to LOTEA, and I were required to report on progress made and on our proposed course of action whenever the seriousness of the occasion warranted it. It was intimidating to say the least to have to appear before such a gathering, but the policy directives which I received, on an essentially private basis, were always reasoned and crystal-clear, and happily normally accorded with my own views. I could then face my own colleagues, and above all the unions, with an overwhelming degree of confidence, to the point where, when some of the more reluctant master stevedore members said 'How can you possibly press on with this or that policy when you are in a minority of one in LOTEA?' I was able to reply: 'One day you'll find out.'

Sir Andrew Crichton was especially concerned with the progress of negotiations, as he was the principal sufferer from the Tilbury ban. I therefore had instructions to 'phone him from time to time to report on how things were going. On one occasion the NASD had thrown a sizeable spanner into the works and put back the prospect of agreement for at least several months. I summoned up my courage to tell Sir Andrew. His reaction was immediate and typical: 'Shall I take the arsenic on my desk?' I suggested that we had a few more meetings to get back on track before he had to do so. Later I was telling this story innocently to some of his shipowner competitors, who did not always see eye-to-eye with Sir Andrew: 'You so-and-so fool,' they told me, 'Why didn't you take your chance and tell him to take it!'

There was one occasion that became a resignation issue for me. As I have already explained, both the shipowners and the employers were split between those who wished to replace the piecework system of payment by an upstanding weekly wage, with only overtime being paid additionally, and those who wished to retain a sizeable element of bonus pay by way of incentive. Ideally the first would have been appropriate to container-ship operations and the second to conventional vessels. However, the trade unions, in pursuance of what they considered to be fairness for all their members, were adamant that whatever system was chosen must apply to all. The TGWU, very much stronger numerically than the NASD, was substantially in favour of the upstanding wage, whereas the NASD preferred bonuses. A choice had to be made, and it was for the employers to decide.

Here the weakness of the employers lay, as always, in their fragmentation. The private master stevedores favoured the payment of one-third of the wages as a bonus incentive. The Port of London Authority operating on their own mechanized berths, were proposing a bonus of as little as 10 per cent. The TGWU used this discrepancy to force the private employers in line with the PLA. Others felt that to retain an incentive of as little as 10 per cent would be no real incentive at all, and would merely encourage the men to retain the piecework attitudes that had been so damaging in the past. The latter view (shared by myself) finally prevailed, and early in 1969 we offered the men an upstanding wage of £32 per week for five seven-hour shifts (two shifts to be worked daily, 7am to 2pm and 2pm to 9pm). Such was the importance of the issue that both the unions, for the first time in their history, put the question of whether or not to accept the Employers' terms to secret ballot.

I recall waiting anxiously at the LOTEA headquarters with my faithful secretary, Douglas Bennett, waiting for the results to come in from the various docks. Many of the employers and some of the shipowners hoped we should be defeated.

We were narrowly beaten: the offer had been rejected. Two courses were open. One was to increase the weekly wage marginally in the hope of winning over more votes. The other – favoured by many, including the largest of the private stevedoring firms – was to use the men's rejection as an excuse to abandon the notion of the upstanding wage and revert to the original concept of a basic wage plus one-third incentive bonus.

I remained unconvinced that the latter idea would be successful, and believed that the unions would reject it. But my views were clearly not acceptable, and the issue was taken to the 'Grannies' Committee'. Evidently a great deal of prior lobbying had been going on.

My friend Toby Jewitt, a most honourable and sincere proponent of the bonus theory, accompanied me. After giving the shipowners my own view, I invited him to expound the alternative. He did so with great ability. In the consequent debate it was evident that a majority of the shipowners wished to follow his advice. I confined myself to making clear what I thought the union reaction to such a *volte face* by the employers might be: I said also that, although I would loyally carry out any direction I received, I could not believe in the success of the policy, and that they might well be better served by choosing a chairman who was more committed to the new line. Toby immediately – and typically – said that he thought that any change of leadership would be a mistake. Sir Nicholas Cayzer intervened to say that, while he fully recognised the strength of my personal conviction, he wished me to stay on and do my best to carry out the shipowners' policy. Even before Sir Nicholas had sat down I had made up my mind that, as their servant, I had no alternative but to do what the majority of the shipowners clearly wished. The final thrust of the sword came when Sir Nicholas was supported by Dennis Martin-Jenkins who, as Chairman of Ellerman Lines and hence of Hovey Antwerp, was effectively my paymaster. My acceptance of the decision was perhaps made easier by the sure knowledge, born of the experience which could be gained only by face-to-face negotiations with the trade-union leaders, that the new policy was not viable and could never be acceptable to the unions as a basis for settlement. Twelve months earlier it might have been, but too much water had by now passed under the bridge.

The conclusion of the matter was that, at least for the time being, the 'container lobby' headed by P&O and OCL had been defeated by the conventional lobby, which consisted of most of the remaining liner shipowners. Sir Andrew gave his clear view that it would be dangerous to change horses in mid-stream, and Sir Donald concluded the meeting somewhat peremptorily. As he left the room he declared to the company at large but, I felt to me in particular: 'It is a pity that force of argument has been outweighed by force of numbers.'

It should, however, be remembered that the British liner shipowners' position was one of extreme difficulty. Nearly all of them had, through one or other of the major consortia, OCL and ACT, made very substantial investments in the untried future represented by the container age, and had yet to get a single penny piece in return. Yet those very investments had been made possible only through their current income from conventional operations, which they thought (with good reason) would be placed in jeopardy by agreements ensuring the success of containerisation at the expense of conventional work. It was a cruel choice to ask them to make, and it is no wonder that voices were raised and counsel divided.

The outcome was, however, entirely predictable. I went back to the trade unions with the employers' new plan, and did my utmost to give a fair wind to Toby Jewitt. He very ably expounded its advantages to those of the men who were eager to retain their previous high earning ability. The trade-union leaders, though, were adamant that they would have none of it. They were quite astute enough to know what had happened behind closed doors, and were quick to give the container lobby the ammunition it needed in the further battle that clearly had to take place. The unions, the leaders said, were now sold on the concept of an upstanding wage, which was right for the containerisation that represented the future for their people. They regretted that, by a narrow majority, the employers' previous proposal had been defeated, and made it clear that, if another two pounds could be added to the weekly wage, they would recommend their members to accept.

Toby Jewitt took this reversal with abundant good grace. The strength of feeling on the unions' side must have been apparent to him. The ban on container work at Tilbury remained the unions' trump card. With a settlement virtually on offer, the choices were between acceptance – with all the uncertainties which this implied for conventional working – and failure to reach any agreement at all – which would have stopped containerisation dead it its tracks and left conventional working in the chaotic downward spiral it had been pursuing for years. In retrospect, I do not regret the shipowners' last sincere attempt to change the tide. Some of their worst predictions about conventional working were fulfilled. It is fair to say that they had known the facts and had made the decisions by which we all stood or fell.

In the event, the inevitable reversion to an upstanding-wage policy went through almost unchallenged. I do not recall any further meeting of the 'Grannies', although a report-back meeting to the shipowners must have been held. Negotiations with the unions were reopened, this time with more money on the table, and agreement was swiftly reached. True to their word, the unions recommended acceptance: at a second secret ballot the membership accepted the employers' financial proposals, which were the cornerstone of Devlin Stage Two. The container ban was lifted forthwith. Sir Andrew was euphoric and the first OCL container ship soon berthed in Tilbury Docks.

What part, if any, did the government play in these substantial events? It was of course essential that they should never be seen to issue instructions, only advice. What happened within the magic circle at the Department of Employment is something we can only guess at. My own guess is that the incumbent Labour administration wanted an agreement that was both in line with union policy and yet economically viable.

Their advice was conveyed through the government's principal conciliation officer, the forerunner of ACAS, Conrad (later Sir Conrad) Heron. One of my most pleasant duties during these difficult times was to meet with Conrad, especially on the occasions when I felt isolated from my colleagues. The meetings were sometimes at his request, sometimes at mine. His fount of wisdom was unfailing, and I invariably left his office feeling strengthened and no longer *alone*. I suppose, in retrospect, that his major quality besides patience, in which he was an expert, was his ability to listen, to sum up and always to have a helpful reply.

Meetings at St James Square were frequently ended by whispered asides and telephone calls between the officials as to the best way to leave the building. Fleet Street was adept at sensing any incipient crisis in the docks, and it was futile to think that one could visit the Department of Employment without the press knowing about it. The art lay in the route of departure. Various subterranean tunnels provided means of escape. One led to Jermyn Street, and there were certainly others. By this means one could, with luck, avoid the attention of the journalists on those occasions when publicity would have done nothing but harm.

Meetings with the heads of the goverment's Labour and Transport departments occurred from time to time. At one the employers' chairman had the temerity to suggest a meeting with Jack Dash in the presence of Ray Gunter, who was Minister of Labour and, while a staunch trade unionist, of right-wing persuasion, Gunter's retort was sharp and swift: he would not be seen dead with Jack Dash, let alone talk to him.

Another recollection concerns Barbara Castle, then Minister of Transport in the Wilson administration. Jack Dash had been organising chaos in the Royal Docks. In an attempt to counter it, John Kiernan and I had invoked the only powers we had under the National Dock Labour Scheme. We suspended all the strikers for five days. The effect was that the Royal Docks were closed for a week. We were summoned by Castle to explain our conduct. She had been exceptionally well briefed (probably by Conrad Heron, who was also present). Over a cup of tea we explained that we were trying to get some discipline back into the docks. Her reply – 'How can you expect to do that, when I can't?' – was disconcerting, to say the least, until one reflected that her far-reaching industrial-relations package, *In Place of Strife,* had just recently been rejected by the government on the grounds that it was unpopular within the trade-union movement. We came away disillusioned, but at least aware that even those in the seats of power have their problems!

The main proposals of Devlin Stage Two had now been delineated, but we still had to draw up a detailed agreement. Particularly, we had to ensure that the NASD was fully identified with the new proposals. Fortunately there were men of good will in both unions – notably Peter Shea of the TGWU and Les Newman of the NASD – who were prepared to put their own reputations at stake during the negotiation of the minutiae of the new deal. This was especially praiseworthy in the case of Les: his office was elective, and his members predominantly of the high-earning bracket and so might be more expected to resist change.

The Joint Modernisation Committee for the enclosed docks, where any agreement would have to be finalised, was an unwieldy and overloaded structure. I had long suggested to Peter Shea, on behalf of the employers, that we should at an appropriate moment form a smaller joint committee, perhaps five-a-side, to hammer out the final details. For several months this suggestion had lain on the table, with Peter unable to obtain the necessary plenipotentiary powers from his union. I chaired a meeting of the Ocean Trades Group Joint Committee in the autumn of 1969. It was a Friday, and I was contemplating a break in the West Country for the following week. Without warning, Peter opened the debate by announcing that the TGWU wished immediately to meet with the employers in the smaller committee in order to reach final agreement on all details of Devlin Two, and that he was mandated to do so on behalf of his union. Les confirmed that he could likewise act for the NASD. I accepted with alacrity, at the same time lamenting in an undertone the loss of my week's holiday in the West Country! Fortunately for me, Walter Lewis, who was sitting beside me, heard my comment. I was later rewarded by a Christmas cruise in the *Andes* for myself and my family.

The five-a-side committee provided a good example of negotiation as it should be. The 10 members acted genuinely as individuals, politics of any kind were put resolutely aside, and we each concentrated on producing a workable agreement that would be acceptable to all. We were treading on wholly new ground, and had really only our wealth of accumulated experience and a fund of good will to guide us.

I was quite determined that we should drive the matter through to conclusion. It was now or never, and so all of us, despite the fact that we were extremely busy, agreed to put aside our other commitments until we had achieved our goal. The PLA lent us an oak-panelled conference room in their palatial offices on Tower Hill. Here we could be secluded and undisturbed, yet secure in the knowledge that detailed advice from colleagues would be readily available. A working lunch was provided daily. It took us three weeks of concentrated discussions to conclude an agreement, the main planks of which were as follows:

- Piecework to be abolished throughout the enclosed docks and replaced by an upstanding weekly wage, payable at all times. The only permissible payments in addition were weekend overtime and awards given on specific salvage operations.
- Shiftwork to be introduced for the first time. Effectively this meant spreading the work available over more people and thus increasing jobs. It also meant increasing the number of hours per day which a ship could work from an estimated average of 6.5 to a nominal 14, with great potential advantage to ship turnround.
- For the first time the unions agreed that a man was to be paid only if actually available for work. Late starts and early finishes, always the bane of dockland, were to be dealt with by deduction of pay.
- Manning scales, a sacred idol of the piecework system, were to go. No longer would a gang refuse to work if it were one or two men short. Work would continue, albeit at a pace commensurate with the reduced manpower.

• Much the most difficult and contentious problem concerned the kind of discipline to be used in the event of men not working at a reasonable speed on a conventional ship. Container ships were no problem – the speed of the machinery dictated the rate of work – but on conventional ships the rate still depended, in the last resort, on the man. Under the piecework system, slow work had automatically meant no more than basic earnings, although these were high enough to content many of the men, particularly those who were 'moonlighting' elsewhere. Any attempt to lay down rates of work for specific commodities would only have brought with it claims for impedence and all the other problems we were were hoping to avoid. The unions were adamant that discipline for misbehaviour, including poor performance, should remain with the National Dock Labour Board, who alone had the power to dismiss a person from the industry. In our hearts we knew that this power would never be taken – indeed, it would have been wholly unreasonable for the trade-union officers, as part of the management team, to have taken such action against their own members. In the end we had to rely on trust and on the fact that each man was now identified with a company which, if it could not work its ships effectively, would go to the wall, with consequent loss of jobs. Looking at the agreement all these years later, I find this last part the one that causes me the most heart searching. Were we justified, in an industry renowned for its lack of trust and mutual responsibility, to take anything on trust? On the other hand, we had to break with the past and step into a new world. Containers were coming apace and change was everywhere. In retrospect, I think our actions were inevitable.

The agreement reached by our committee was duly ratified during a formal signing ceremony at the employers' headquarters, followed by a proper celebration – although not before I had had to deal with minor alterations to the wording. Dealing separately with Peter Shea and Les Newman, I had had to find words or often just nuances that would be acceptable to both of their unions. The NASD played hard-to-get – to the end – they were half an hour late for the ceremony – but in the end everyone signed. That document is a treasured possession.

What had we achieved in London? Certainly the port would never be the same again. Today its size has diminished out of all recognition. St Katharine's, London Dock, the Surreys, West India, Millwall and the Royals are silent. But this would have happened anyway, with the increasing size of vessels and the switch to containers. What we did when forging this agreement almost certainly accelerated the process, and played a vital part in inaugurating the 'Container Age'. Predictably, conventional work became very difficult, and this perhaps hastened the transition to containers, while costing the shipowner a great deal of money at a critical time.

The new agreement was followed not by a period of peace and gratitude for the conditions which had been won but by one of strife, much of it political. It is difficult to know to what extent the agreement itself was responsible. The employers using conventional ships reported varying experiences. Several smaller firms that had always fostered a sense of mutual respect, and where close employer-employee relations were the order of the day, prospered and were able to improve their productivity because in this way the men protected their jobs and in due course could be rewarded by a share of the firm's profitability. Inside the large firms, however, although there was good will in high places, junior managers had become so inured to dealing with the depressing problems of trying to keep a dying piecework system going that they had in effect lost both the knowledge and the will to manage. In the worst cases, the relationship between employer and employed was so poor, and the lack of trust so great, that no agreement could have been devised to build a permanent bridge.

Nevertheless, although minor amendments have been made and a minimal bonus incentive rightly introduced, the basic Devlin Stage Two agreement remains intact. The fact that, for what is left of the Port of London, it has stood the test of time is perhaps the best testimony both to it and to those who so painstakingly negotiated it.

SOUTHAMPTON

1 Out of the frying pan into the fire

It was during the final stages of the negotiations over Devlin Stage Two that I came face to face with my own future. For the best part of four years I had been involved in the top decision and policy-making of the industry, and had had little time for my family business (although it had continued to pay me a salary). 1970 was a year in which politics in the port industry were very much in the ascendant. The Labour government of the day had as one of its main objectives the nationalisation of the ports. This included the acquisition of all 'port businesses' and would therefore spell the end of our family stevedoring company. Faced with this possibility, and in view of the part which I had been called on to play in the preceding few years, the idea of joining the proposed National Ports Authority or one of its local offshoots had a certain attraction. Had the opportunity been offered, I might well have accepted it. On several occasions I briefed myself by going to Westminster and listening to the debate on the Ports Bill, which was intended to give effect to the nationalisation programme.

However, luckily for me, fate decreed otherwise. In the event the government had to abandon the Ports Bill owing to the narrowness of its majority in the House and the abstention of two Labour MPs in a critical vote. Shortly afterwards the administration was defeated at a general election; the incoming conservative government had no interest in port nationalisation.

In the meantime I had received an approach from David Lloyd suggesting that I apply for the post of general manager of a new terminal-operating company at Southampton, which had been chosen by both Overseas Containers and Ben Line Containers as their British port for the handling of the Far East container trade. This trade was perhaps the largest and most lucrative of those operated by the British Shipowners. It was dominated by P&O and Blue Funnel, although other companies, such as Ben Line and Ellermans, had a substantial share. The trade was to be run as part of a consortium including the West German and Japanese lines (it came to be known as Trio Lines), and in this form it constituted the largest and most valuable trading link in the world.

It was an offer I found hard to refuse, especially since I had a high regard for both Sir Andrew Crichton, the Chairman of Overseas Containers, who I already knew from his connection with the port industry, and for David Lloyd, of Ellermans, who had made the suggestion. Terms were arranged, and within days I was in a small office near St Mary Axe, along with a minimal staff of experts who had been recruited to carry out a feasibility study into a Southampton Terminal.

Sir Andrew had given me clear and explicit instructions to turn Southampton into Britain's premier container port. I asked him if I could visit other world ports that had faced the problems I would have to face. Armed with a first-class round-the-world ticket and fortified by the frequent glasses of champagne that accompanied it, I made a three-week trip to Australia, Hong Kong, Japan and the western and eastern seaboards of the United States. As it proved, little of this experience had a direct bearing on the Southampton problem, but I did get an interesting overview of the widely differing national reactions to that same old problem: how to move from labour-intensive conventional cargo-handling systems to that of the container and the sophisticated machine, in which one or two men were required in place of the 10 formerly employed, and yet to do so with a minimum of disruption and without compromising the cost-efficiency of the new systems.

Before I was to get to grips with my evaluation, I had a further encounter with Sir Andrew. I had travelled direct to Australia (with short stopovers at New York, Los Angeles, Hawaii and Fiji) and arrived in Sydney at about 8am, then being escorted to my hotel. I slept until late afternoon. The next day, at 9am, I reported at OCAL's office in Bridge Street. I was in the process of talking to one of their directors when who should come in but Sir Andrew. I had no idea whatsoever that he was in Australia, and he had evidently forgotten that I was. The conversation was direct and to the point.

'What are you doing here?' he said.

'You sent me, sir.'

'When did you arrive?'

'Yesterday morning, sir.'

'Go back to bed at once. You should have two days' rest after that journey!'

Such was the measure of the man. I always found Sir Andrew to be considerate in the extreme.

It was as well that I went to Australia first. OCL and ACT had been operating with containers there for about two years. Terminals had been set up at White Bay in Sydney and at Swanson Dock in Melbourne. I visited both of these ports, as well as Brisbane, arriving at the beginning of December 1970. Virtually no work had been in progress in either Sydney or Melbourne for some six weeks. One after another, various sections of Australian port labour had gone on strike, leaving the others unable to work but having nevertheless to be paid, and the entire port system paralysed. Management was clearly at the end of its tether. I discovered the cruellest cut of all when I arrived at Melbourne: the cooks on the tugs were on strike. There were only a few of these cooks but their strike meant the tugs were unable to move and therefore the ships were unable to sail.

All this was unhappily reminiscent of the worst abuses of the piecework system in post-war London. Management and men appeared totally at odds with one another, and little effort seemed to be being made to bridge the gap. It looked as if the mechanics of containerisation had been imposed on an industrial framework which reflected all the worst confrontational attitudes, and in which no suggestion of a common aim or purpose had been sought. It is said that, when White Bay Terminal was opened, the resistance to change was so great that, from the housing estate on a bluff overlooking the terminal, dead cats were thrown and even shots fired at the personnel. All of this did not augur well for the success of my task at Southampton. (It is a sad reflection on that part of the world that, on a recent revisit to Australian waters, I found the situation little improved.)

From Sydney I flew to Hong Kong, where I was met at Kai Tek by 'Monty' Monteith, OCL's Technical Director. We spent only one day in Hong Kong, but it was enough to sense the vibrancy and excitement of the place. The container port at Kwaichung was under construction.

Typically, the Hong Kong authorities had ignored the existence of the old wharves, which in any event had no available hinterland for containers, and had created a new port by the simple expedient of excavating the tops of nearby mountains and casting them into the bay. A new technique, a new world and a brand new port to accommodate it! Fortunately for Hong Kong, the Chinese work ethic was such as to ensure also the necessary change of attitudes. Hong Kong has never looked back.

From Hong Kong, Monty and I flew to Japan, where we visited the ports of Tokyo and Kobe. By and large, the philosophy was the same as in Hong Kong. The situation in Kobe was especially interesting. Kobe is the port for Osaka, and was a major conventional port. Rather than adapt it for container purposes, which could well have been possible, the Japanese had employed the Hong Kong technique, simply cutting off the top of a nearby mountain and dumping it into the bay to create a man-made island surrounded by water deep enough to berth any container ship then contemplated. Known as Port Island, this artefact exemplified the far-sightedness and willingness to face change head-on which seemed to me typical of the Far East.

From Japan we headed for the United States, where we were greeted with typical hospitality. Both in San Francisco and later in New Jersey's Port Elizabeth, then the world's largest container port, we found a very different situation. I suspected then, and afterwards verified, that the basic labour situation had changed little from the old days. Employment of the men was to a large extent on a casual basis, but the union bosses were extremely strong and able to deliver, sometimes by dubious means, whatever the shipowners required... provided always that the price was right.

The Americans had built a first-class mechanical infrastructure, and nothing had been spared in the creation of modern mechanised facilities, but at the same time they had left the basic human situation very much as before. On the west coast they had introduced the famous West Coast Agreement, negotiated in a 'goldfish bowl' because otherwise it would have been less likely to be acceptable to the men. By means of huge payments into union-controlled pension funds, the employers had ostensibly 'bought the book' on restrictive practices in container operations and reduced the manning scales. But the element of casualism, and thus casual attitudes, remained and was reflected in what one of the

US stevedoring company executives told me: 'Every three or four years we have to have a ritual blood-letting to enable the unions to gain a victory and re-establish their control for another few years.'

On the east coast was an even more 'we and they' situation. So far as I could see, the numbers of dockers had not been reduced, and the price to be paid for one man to drive a container crane was the same as the wages of the 17 men who would previously have done the job, and who were now being paid for doing virtually nothing. In short, the Americans had bought their way into containerisation at a substantial price.

England was cold and damp on our return. At once I had to put aside the problems of London, where the future of the container business was now assured, and concentrate on the particular problems of Southampton.

My earlier experience with Hovey Antwerp at Tilbury convinced me that the only way to make a modern container operation successful was to establish an entirely separate operating unit, employing its own staff and labour in the numbers strictly necessary for the work to be performed. Somehow people had to be weaned from their old loyalties: a new relationship, based on the economic viability of the operation and thus on the welfare of both employer and employee, had to be established. At Tilbury, where the dockers had always had a tradition of independence from the rest of London, this concept had been well received. I was fortified by the recent experience of my world tour, in which it had been clear to me that, in those countries (such as Hong Kong and Japan, and to some degree the United States) where the shipowners had been able to break free from former constraints, container operations were a success. Where the shipowners had failed to change the old traditional industrial infrastructure, and had merely superimposed the new mechanical operations, as was very evident in Australia, then little but chaos had resulted. In sum, it was all a question of attitude. With good reason, given their past history of insecurity and exploitation, dockers tended to be defensive, suspicious of change and above all wedded to the rule books and to the ultimate weapon – the strike – enshrined under British law as their only and latterly very effective defence. Somehow this situation had to be turned around so that employees would see it to be in their best interests to work well for a company with which they could be closely identified, and of which they could feel a part – not just financially but also in terms of 'belonging to a family'. The turnaround would have to be accomplished, it seemed, in two stages: first, by administrative action defining and separating off the new employing unit; second, by sheer management ability used to lead and persuade people, over a period of years, to forsake the old sterile attitudes in favour of the new.

Solent Container Services, the terminal operating company for the port of Southampton, was set up in December 1970. My first chairman was Pat Tobin, a man whom I came almost to revere. From a military background, he was one of the half a dozen or so founding directors of OCL. 65% of Solent Container Services' equity was held by OCL and the remainder by Ben Line and Ellermans, who were partners in the ACT consortium. OCL and ACT were, of course, in competition with one another as container shipowners, and I used sometimes to reflect that, with such a division of ownership, it was difficult to be wholly wrong! My board was laced with members who had themselves had first-hand experience in dealing with dock labour, and such was the importance accorded to this subject – quite rightly, in my view – that a very substantial part of our board's time used to be consumed by it. I had no hesitation whatsoever in recommending to Sir Andrew Crichton and to my chairman and board that, if they wished to ensure the success of the Southampton operation, SCS must be set up as an entirely separate operating company within the port of Southampton, employing its own personnel, devising its own policies, being financially independent, and standing or falling on its own merit. My board agreed unanimously that this policy was sound, and I still think it would probably have succeeded, within a few years, in turning Southampton – as Sir Andrew wished – into Britain's premier container port.

But I had reckoned without the situation at Southampton. The shipowners had of course committed themselves to the port some time before SCS was formed, and had entered into agreements with the British Transport Docks Board, who owned and operated Southampton as one of the 19 ports which they had inherited largely as a result of the nationalisation of the railways after the war. Construction of Southampton's container terminal had already started, and undertakings had been given by the British shipowners to their German and Japanese counterparts that operations there would begin on time. With their memories still focused on Tilbury and the international embarrassment and expense they had suffered through having to send their ships to Antwerp, and with the Trio Lines' vessels scheduled to be delivered from January 1972 onwards, it is no wonder that the question of timing came to play a major part in what followed.

The shipowners had quite correctly chosen Southampton largely because of its natural advantages. With its fine deep-water lock-free port, where the famous double high water provided access at most stages of the tide, Southampton lay directly on the route from the Far East to the northern Continental ports. In addition, and most importantly, it was well connected by rail to the industrial heartlands of London, the Midlands and northern England. Moreover, linking motorways were planned. All in all it seemed that a perfect site had been chosen. Remarkably little seems to have been said during this formative period of decision-making about industrial relations at Southampton – something all the more remarkable because Union Castle (a part of the British and Commonwealth Group, who were partners in OCL) had long been major users of the port. What was abundantly evident, however, was an overwhelming desire by the British shipowners and their German and Japanese colleagues – all of whom had previously divided their conventional services between London and Liverpool – to escape from the clutches of the two ports which had caused them so much expense and damage, particularly during the latter years of the piecework system.

The final and perhaps conclusive reason for the choice of Southampton lay in the size of the vessels themselves. Third-generation container vessels, the largest then afloat or contemplated, measured 59,000 displacement tons and had a length of 950ft (290m) and a beam of 108ft (33m). With their maximum draught of 42ft (13m) when laden, their choices of port were strictly limited. For example, Felixstowe, now beginning to establish a first-class reputation, had neither the depth of water nor the facilities required. It could well be argued – and certainly this was a factor that bore heavily in the years ahead – that these ships had nowhere else to go but Southampton.

Before the war Southampton had established its fine reputation as a passenger port, primarily on the Atlantic Trades and especially as the British terminal for Cunard. The port was thus dominated by passenger-ship requirements. It was owned and managed by the Southern Railway, and the ships had to conform to what were virtually railway timetables. A story I am sure is apocryphal (although it contains more than a grain of truth) is that, if a crane driver tried to blackmail his employers by working slowly on loading baggage the day before the *Queen Mary* departed, and his employers declined to submit to that blackmail, then the chairman of Cunard would swiftly be on the telephone to the port manager: 'How dare you hold my ship up? Pay the man at once.' We reap the rewards of our own actions.

After World War II, with the gradual demise of the transatlantic passenger ships, pride of place was taken by the Union Castle Line, which had a regular weekly mail service to South Africa as well as an intermediate service to South and East African ports. Scarcely a week passed without several of the company's vessels being on berth in the Western Docks. On average the line employed almost half of the labour in Southampton. The ships worked to a fixed timescale – 'sailing out of Southampton every Thursday at 4pm'. All the difficulties associated with that dictum were to haunt us in years to come.

The more one delved into the Southampton scene the more apparent became the differences from London. To begin with, Southampton was physically a much smaller port. London was so huge that, in spite of the intense loyalty among the dockers, there had always been enough of them for rivalry and separation to exist between the various dock groups. Because of the multiplicity of employers and the popularity of the gang system, particularly in the piecework days, the men were accustomed to working in small units and being rewarded accordingly. It is significant that at Tilbury there was little problem in negotiating special terms and conditions for specialist berths, which brought higher rewards although for only a limited number of men: the sole problem lay in persuading the unions to allow these special agreements to be operated through guaranteeing a high enough minimum wage for the remainder of the men. In short, in London the 'family unit' was never the port as a whole. At Southampton matters were quite different. One could visit every berth on a bicycle in under an hour! The dockers all belonged to one union branch, not several as in London. Above all, although Southampton had been a piecework port as far as general cargo was concerned, the importance of the 'gang' system seems never to have been as central. Perhaps this was because of the extent of baggage-handling, essentially an unskilled individual operation. And this almost certainly accounted also for the pathological addiction to equality which was fundamental to the Southampton dockworkers' thinking. In a small port like Southampton, where everyone knew everyone else, it required no particular perspicacity to realise that the contents of the weekly wage packet were regulated less by effort (or its lack) than by the individual generosity or miserliness of the passengers whose baggage was being handled. Whatever the validity of my theory, the doctrine of equality played a central role in Southampton's future.

Following years of inequity, during which there had been blatant discrimination between one man and the next, equality was a noble and understandable objective. London had solved it, as we have seen, by agreeing to pay an upstanding weekly wage sufficient for any man to support his family comfortably, while also leaving opportunities for overtime. The basic agreement had allowed the container agreements for special groups of workers to go forward, rewarding longer hours and more specialised skills with more money. The dockers at Southampton, by contrast, insisted on complete equality for all – not just equality of earnings but also equality of workload. Southampton had abandoned piecework under the Devlin Stage Two agreement (shortly before the same happened in London) and had established an upstanding wage. But in Southampton's case any available overtime had to be equally shared by all of the men, over quite a short period, and the men had to have an equal share of the lighter and harder work, including that with a mechanical content. This was only possible, however, if all the dockers were managed as one large pool and allocated to work daily not according to their ability but according to the equality criteria. The local Dock Labour Board therefore employed people called port labour officers who had acquired a 'neutral' status and whose duties, as far as I could see, were relevant not so much to the efficiency of the port as to the target of equality which the two sides had set themselves.

Obviously there was a basic conflict between my conception of what was good for Southampton's future and Southampton's own judgement. I remember remarking to a colleague at that time: 'Nothing can stop Southampton's progress except Southampton.' I still see no reason to retract that remark.

It seemed to me imperative that the established system be broken and that SCS should employ all its labour itself. The law of the land dictated that, if one wished to become an employer in dockland, one must apply for and gain a licence that would not be granted unless certain clear criteria were met: financial viability, ability to provide continuous employment for a fixed number of men, willingness to provide amenities, etc. These criteria we were admirably placed to meet, and when I wrote our application I felt (and still do) that ours was the perfect case. In fairness, the timing was less favourable. In the wake of Devlin Stage Two and the resulting difficulties in carrying out conventional operations, the private employers were going out of business one after another, the men being absorbed by the relevant port authorities. We, by contrast, wished to take men away from the Port Authority of Southampton, so that in effect we were swimming against the tide. Before submitting the application officially to the British Transport Docks Board, the licensing authority for the port, I decided to test the water myself. Because we met the criteria so closely I felt sure (especially after a little encouragement from the government department responsible) that our licence must be granted, whatever the views of the Southampton management. The difficulty was going to lie with the unions.

I wrote a concise account of what we proposed to do and why we wanted to employ our own men, and took it to my friend Tim O'Leary at the TGWU headquarters in Smith Square. He was the national official for all the TGWU dockers, and as such was in a position of much influence. I was surprised at the modesty of his accommodation. He read the document with interest and stated quite clearly and openly that he could not disagree with a word of it. But then he added, looking at me somewhat quizzically: 'I think you'd better go down to Southampton and show it to Ernie Allen.' A few days later, in Southampton, I was received by Ernie at his far more palatial office in London Road. Ernie was TGWU regional officer for the south of England, and clearly had a special affinity for and interest in Southampton docks. One of his greatest ambitions had been to introduce an apprenticeship scheme for the workers there, to be jointly funded by the employers and the National Dock Labour Board. He had been thwarted by inter-port politics: the board, dominated by London and Liverpool, declined to support a scheme which would have given Southampton a head-start. Had he succeeded in this far-sighted enterprise the acceptance of the specialisation so necessary to container operations – in the event so stubbornly resisted – could have been considerably eased.

Ernie was a trade-union officer of great intelligence. Not long before he had been responsible for negotiating the Fawley agreements, hailed as a breakthrough in modern industrial history. He had been the driving force behind the abolition of piecework in Southampton, much as Peter Shea had been in London. Ernie read my paper, remained silent rather longer than Tim, and then likewise remarked that he could find nothing to disagree with. Then he added: 'We aren't half going to have trouble with the shop stewards.'

Southampton, a much smaller port than London, had originally been a railway port in which all the responsible jobs, such as superintending, checking and crane driving were performed by Southern Railway employees, members of either the TSSA (for management and clerical grades) or the NUR. The hard graft of fetching and carrying on the quay and in the ships was carried out by TGWU dockers, employed by one or two private contractors and in every way very much second-class citizens. Years passed before the 'peak cap' syndrome, implying the superiority of the railway grades, disappeared. In addition to these unions there were the various engineering unions whose members maintained the equipment.

By the time of my arrival the British Transport Docks Board had become direct employers of all except the TGWU dockers, who were employed by the Southampton Cargo Handling Company, an organisation jointly owned by the BTDB and some remaining private interests, notably the Union Castle Line. Now that mechanised cargo handling, particularly containerisation, was here, the dockers were working with very sophisticated equipment and, although Devlin Stage Two had gone some way towards improving their status, it was still very much the case that – particularly in the eyes of the ex-railwaymen – they remained second-class citizens.

The other important factor to become swiftly evident was that, with the advent of Devlin Stage Two, management and trade unions had understandably decided to try to put the adversarial past behind them (in the immediate pre-Devlin years Southampton had had one of the worst records for stoppages of any port) and in industrial matters to manage the port on a joint basis. Largely through the influence of Ernie Allen, the TGWU were beginning to predominate. They were helped in this by the fact that the National Dock Labour Scheme provided for their members a security of employment which was not available to the other dock workers. Alas, the real authority on the trade-union side was increasingly passed from the paid officials to the elected shop stewards. Ernie Allen, himself the height of responsibility and far-sightedness, had to deal with a wide area, extending far outside dockland, and was an extremely busy man. Official union representation in the docks themselves was unfortunately not strong, and the execution of trade-union policy was being left more and more to the stewards. The process was no doubt assisted by Jack Jones's dictum that all authority originated from the rank-and-file members, who of course elected the shop stewards.

For whatever reason, by the time I arrived in the port Ernie rarely interfered in the day-to-day management of industrial issues, and the port managers were left with little alternative but to deal directly with the stewards. While these latter remained dedicated to the well-being of the Port there was of course no problem, but the system was to have dire consequences in the years ahead.

The one remaining factor that impinged strongly on our efforts to employ our own labour was the fact that BTDB had two years earlier, in 1968, constructed the first container terminal in Southampton. It had been a speculative venture on the boards' part at a time when containerisation was in its infancy and its industrial implications as yet unclear. No doubt the port management was anxious to launch the new operation in such a way as not to disrupt the Union Castle services, which continued to provide employment for 50 per cent of the workforce and thus to dominate the port. It was thus in the interests of both the shipowners and the port authority to introduce the new methods with as little trauma as possible; this accorded perfectly with the trade-union insistence that the equality provisons enshrined in Devlin Stage Two must be preserved at all costs. It is therefore not surprising that the BTDB container berths 201/2 came to be operated as (from an industrial standpoint) an extension of the old conventional systems. There was a minimal recognition of the specialised nature of the operation. The chance to drive the new straddle carriers had to be offered to virtually every docker in the port, on the basis that all must have equal opportunity. Worse still, the 24-hour shift work meant that overtime had to be allocated fairly between every man in the port. The result was that men found themselves operating a straddle-carrier one day, unloading fruit from a Union Castle liner the next, and then perhaps tackling passenger baggage on the third. The issues of separation, creating a special 'family unit', and full recognition for the specialist nature of containerisation were never faced. Nevertheless, the berth had prospered to a degree, since it had then had few competitors and was the British base for two transatlantic lines. It was very much in the interests of both the port management and the unions that the principles on which its operations were founded should not be challenged.

Such was the scenario at the time of my first meeting with Ernie Allen at Southampton. The next step was to make an official application for an employer's licence. Although it was quite evident that there would be rough water ahead, there was no drawing back: this was an issue of principle. The licensing authority was the BTDB. Our case was so good that, in the last resort, it could not have been rejected. There was no provision in the legislation for the licensing authority to take account of union opinion (however well that might be known). We were potentially an important customer, bringing new business worth many millions of pounds to the port.

The BDTB must have been in an unpleasant quandary. It knew something that had certainly never been revealed to us – although it would emerge quite clearly later. The port management had at some stage entered into a tacit understanding that from now on there would be only a single employer of dockers in the port, the Southampton Cargo Handling Company. No doubt the BDTB also felt, with some justification, that what was good enough for its berths should be good enough for ours.

There was also a good deal of dubiety about the role which SCS were expected to play in the port, and no reference had been made to the company in the 'Heads of Agreement' drawn up by OCL/ACT and BTDB. However, Sir Andrew Crichton had told me emphatically that it was my specific responsibility to turn Southampton into a first-class container port, and that he would deny me nothing by way of expertise or financial provision in order to achieve this. There was to be no question of compromise or acceptance of second-best.

I persisted in my application for an employer's licence. I presented it personally to the secretary of the BTDB at the headquarters behind Marylebone Station (redolent of the railways), and he received it with a good grace, although for many months he must have been concerned and embarrassed by its presence on his desk.

The next move was to come to grips directly with the unions, among whom the central opposition to our application would certainly lie. So far as the TGWU was concerned, the matter was relatively easy. Ernie Allen had been convinced from the outset of the rightness of our proposals (he told me later that the great tragedy of Southampton was that the proposals were not forced through). He was equally aware of my determination and the total opposition of his stewards. Ernie called them together so that I could address them. Whether it was out of respect for Ernie or because here was a customer offerring several hundred jobs and a doubling of the ports throughput I do not know, but they listened in respectful silence as I outlined our plans and my conviction that the operation could be successful only if we employed the men ourselves. I stressed the advantages we could bring to the port and to the men we employed. To their questions as to why we could not follow the existing precedents in Southampton, I responded by insisting that, with an operation of our magnitude and with such a high level of efficiency required by the shipowners, this would never work. In retrospect I am sure that they thought of the size of the vessels and noted that construction of the berths had already begun; however, they wisely held their counsel and listened politely. They were well aware of the issues but, as in London, we – the employers – were prisoners of history. Just as in London, inequality had been so rampant and exploitation so rife during the pre-Devlin days that, now that equality had been achieved, it was not to be discarded, however plausible the arguments.

To meet with the other union interests, it was necessary to ask for the help of the management of the BTDB, the direct employers. Dennis Noddings, then docks manager, and I met the various negotiating committees separately. Two committees represented the NUR, one of the crane drivers (the elite of industrial Southampton) and one for the checkers; the TSSA represented lower and middle grades of management, including superintendents; the Allied Trades represented engineering and maintenance workers; last but not least came the foremen, some of whom belonged to the TGWU and supervised their docker members, whilst others belonged to the TSSA, so that there was a kind of dual authority at the lowest level of management.

It was to this rather motley brigade that Dennis and I addressed ourselves. In every case we were received with courtesy, and I was able to expound my views and intentions, assuring them of our willingness to employ their members in the appropriate numbers. I then outlined to them how I saw the port developing over the months and years ahead. In each case the result was the same: not outright antagonism, rather a kind of incredulous disbelief. Eyes glazed over, and I am sure that they were thinking: 'Who does he think he is? The man from Mars? Doesn't he realize that this is Southampton?' But the union representatives were without exception models of courtesy, and remained so throughout my dealings with them. What also became apparent during my talks with Dennis Noddings was that, although – provided a licence was granted – our direct employment of dockers presented no problem, in the case of the others, because they were all BTDB staff members, a series of complicated negotiations would be required.

At this stage the omens were not encouraging, but the issues were so important that there was no question of giving in. We were fortified in our resolution by the increasing certainty that the type of operation carried out at 201/2 berths would result in a disastrous collapse if applied to our own berths.

Meanwhile SCS was establishing itself at Southampton. I had moved into a small office opposite Donald Stringer, the director of the port, in Dock House. This was a substantial privilege, and one accorded to few if any other 'outsiders'; it no doubt reflected our importance as customers.

My first official function in Southampton was to accompany Donald to the annual New Year Shipping service at the Mission to Seamen, a function attended by all those concerned in the welfare of the port. Donald was kind enough to introduce me to the Master Mariners Club, perhaps the most prestigious social meeting place in the port. I was glad to join, although I perhaps disappointed Donald in that I rarely crossed its portals until much later, when SCS had become well established at Southampton.

The problem was typical of those we were to face. SCS was an untried collection of individuals, dedicated to a new method of operation. The Master Mariners Club, as its name indicated, was composed mainly of people who had spent their lives at sea, and to whom the hallowed traditions of Southampton as a passenger port were sacrosanct. Southampton had a proud and famous history, and the club enshrined the establishment, whose interest was to foster and if possible preserve the image of the port as they had known and loved it. The problem was that it was changing before their eyes: we had been sent from London with a commission to bring about a revolution that would alter the character of the port forever. No wonder we were not exactly popular.

I felt that, if I were to have any chance at all of fulfilling my commission, I must – while paying proper respect to the glories of the past – avoid the master mariners' embrace like the plague itself. That is perhaps why, at a very early stage, instead of indulging myself whenever opportunity offered itself at the fleshpots of the establishment in the port area, I tended to patronise pubs and hotels on the edge of the New Forest.

We moved into our excellent new office, built to our order by BTDB in the centre of the new terminal, in the early summer of 1971, after a short period at Imperial House in the Western Docks, formerly used by Imperial Airways in connection with their flying-boat services. Unlike BTDB's terminal at 201/2, berths 204/5 were built to the specific instruction of OCL and ACT, representing the British shipowners. Although the terminal infrastructure and the three massive Portainer cranes were to be the property of BTDB, they were effectively paid for by an annual charge spread over the 20 years of the agreement. OCL/ACT were to have the sole use of the berths, and were therefore able to dictate the types of equipment to be used. Under the terms of the agreement, once SCS was established the rights of OCL/ACT devolved on the new company.

The construction of the berths, which continued through 1971 and 1972, was a triumph of engineering skill. A vast trench was dredged in the upper reaches of Southampton Water where the River Test debouched into it. The sand and gravel thus recovered were pumped onto an area to be reclaimed, which was enclosed to seaward by a wall of steel piles 80ft (24m) long, driven into the chalk bedrock of the river. Our offices, in these early months, stood on a gravel island in the midst of a sea of excavation and reclamation, gravel and mud. It was fascinating to watch an area which I had first known as the haunt of thousands of seabirds being slowly transformed into one of the finest container terminals in the world. (A less happy recollection is that, in later years, when the terminal was strike-bound and idle, the birds returned in equal numbers to reclaim – temporarily – their own.)

Unfortunately, virtually nothing had been said in the agreement with BTDB about the human side of the operation. OCL/ACT made the decision to set up what they described as an operating company of their own. My own terms of reference as general manager of SCS made it very clear that I was to be solely responsible for the conduct of the Southampton operation, financially and in every other way. This intention had been notified to the port management but may well have come as a surprise – or even a bitter blow to the port authority: at the time of the signing of the agreement, the authority must have regarded itself as the only body with the ability to perform these functions. Now, though, another organisation was growing steadily and obviously intended to provide the management structure. With its declared aim of separating berths 204/5 completely from the remainder of the port and taking labour presently employed by BTDB in order to operate the new berths as a separate entity, SCS obviously represented a threat. No wonder that in some quarters we must have been looked upon as a cuckoo in the nest: it is a tribute to all concerned that we were always received with considerable courtesy.

The summer months of 1971 ran on. The deadline for the completion of all the arrangements and the arrival of the first Japanese vessel was early 1972. Construction of the berths proceeded apace; SCS's recruitment and training of management personnel was in full swing; and sophisticated machinery, in the form of straddle carriers to be owned by SCS, began to arrive. On the labour front, by contrast, little stirred. Our licence application lay on BTDB's desk at Melbury House in London. They must surely have known that, barring any unheralded outside intervention, they would have to grant it; yet their management at the Southampton level must also have known the possible difficulties within the port that the granting of the license might bring – problems that could jeopardise the BTDB's own operations at berths 201/2 as well as Southampton's Union Castle business.

All sorts of pressures were brought to bear on me – albeit in the kindest possible way – to reconsider my decision. Many conceded that in theory I was right but that in practice what I wanted was the impossible. Nevertheless, I remained convinced that, if Sir Andrew's commission was to be fulfilled, we could not yield. It was a matter of principle, and on this my board supported me. Yet against me I had not only the trade unions but also the interests of the BTDB management, Union Castle and the Southampton establishment.

I continued to talk with the various groups of trade unionists – the BTDB and the Cargo Handling Company provided every assistance on this – but the impasse continued. I was adamant that it was in *their* interests that we should employ our own people. Any other course would provide our customers with shoddy service. The unions, their sacred cow of equality threatened, were courteous but never ceased to point out the potential difficulties.

In the end, the issue was resolved in a way which I had come to know well in dockland and which, although I could never approve, I came to understand. Ernie Allen was besieged in his office one afternoon by a crowd of angry shop stewards. They had reached the conclusion that this newcomer from London was not going to take their wise advice to withdraw, and that the BTDB might be forced to concede the licence. Ernie was in a quandary. Whatever his own private views at the time (in later years he had no doubt that our decision to press for a licence was the right one), he had to deal with an immediate crisis. He knew that the stewards had valid grounds for their grievance, in that a licence for us to employ men directly would breach the tacit understanding that there would be only one employer in the port. He also knew that, if we were given a licence, both the BTDB and the other shipowning interests in Southampton, including Union Castle, would probably suffer the adverse effects of immediate industrial unrest – if not a complete stoppage. There might even be a national dock strike.

Ernie picked up the telephone to Sir Andrew Crichton in London and suggested that he come to Southampton and intervene personally in a situation which, in Ernie's view, was rapidly getting out of hand and could lead to major problems for the shipowners. Ernie subsequently apologised to me for going over my head, but his action was perhaps understandable in the light of the circumstances.

The meeting at Southampton a few days later was dramatic in the extreme, and dictated the course of events in Southampton for many years to come. Sir Andrew was accompanied by Michael Strachan, the Chairman of Ben Line Containers. The BTDB was represented by Donald Stringer. I and the manager of the Cargo Handling Company completed the employers' side. For the workers, Ernie Allen was accompanied by his docks officer, Sam Hocking, and by two of his most senior shop stewards.

At once it became clear that the TGWU were the moving spirits behind the meeting. The venue – chosen by Ernie Allen – was an unlikely but perhaps, for Southampton, typical one: the Mecca restaurant at the end of the Royal Pier. Built in the era of Queen Victoria's visits to Osborne, Isle of Wight, the pier and particularly the restaurant were redolent of that age. Both the meeting room and the room where Ernie subsequently hosted a luncheon, with Sir Andrew and Michael Strachan flanking him, were awash with gilt and red plush, a monument to a bygone age.

I was given every opportunity to outline my plans and the reasons why I felt it was in everybody's long-term interests for us to conduct an independent operation employing its own people. Ernie and his colleagues listened courteously, and were at pains to stress the sincerity of my views. However, (and this was not my fault), I did not know Southampton as well as they did. Ernie diplomatically left it to his colleagues to elaborate on the dire consequences if I were allowed to have my way. Donald, on behalf of the BTDB, wisely held his peace, no doubt knowing the ambiguity of the BTDB's position.

Ernie then played his trump card. We were all reasonable men. The unions shared my determination that the operation should be a complete success, but in their view it was possible to achieve this without breaking the one-employer concept. They were certain that in discussion with me they could satisfy me on all points concerning the efficiency of the operation, and pledged themselves to that effect. We had a recess, and I had to tell the shipowners that, if we agreed to anything less than direct employment, 100 per cent efficiency would never be obtained. If we settled for the compromise seemingly on offer – that a number of individuals employed by the Southampton Cargo Handling Company and by the BTDB should be seconded to SCS for a substantial period – then, given the ability of the trade-union leaders to deliver their promises, we could perhaps achieve at best 75 per cent efficiency.

The BTDB continued to hold its peace, possibly because it knew that it, too, had a financial axe to grind in preserving the one-employer concept (as we were subsequently to discover). At any event, the BTDB made no attempt to influence our decision, apart from confirming that the union suggestion was indeed a practical one.

I think in retrospect that the shipowners' minds may have been made up before they came to Southampton. Sir Andrew, particularly, had had unhappy experiences with the container-berth men at Tilbury who, although in the employ of the PLA, were a fixed group of individuals and to all intents and purposes the servants of OCL. Perhaps because of this memory, Sir Andrew was well aware of the 'How do you get rid of the rotten apple in the barrel?' argument. Perhaps there was merit in the practice of leaving the employment of labour with someone else, with a degree of 'rotation' through the workforce which would resolve the 'rotten apple' problem.

Whatever the reasons, the decision was quickly made and did not at all surprise me. The pressures were very strong, and it would have been a bold man who plunged Southampton (and possibly other ports) into chaos in pursuit of aims whose attainability, by their very nature, had yet to be proved. The shipowners accepted that the dockers, and by extension every other worker in the port, would continue to be employed either by the Southampton Cargo Handling Company or by BTDB, with the provision that the TGWU were able to satisfy me on the issue of efficiency. Until the union had done so – and meetings were to begin forthwith – our application for a licence would remain lodged with BTDB. The stewards did not like that part of it, but it was to prove an effective weapon in the months ahead, and without it the end result would have been even worse than in the event it was.

Clearly the TGWU negotiation was the key one: there was little point in considering the other BTDB employees until the dockers' issue had been thrashed out. It was quickly apparent that the question of rotation of labour in order to share out available earnings, particularly overtime, on the basis of equality between all the men lay at the root of the problem. Subject only to this, the union leaders were sincere in their promises to provide the 24-hour coverage we needed and to have men available and trained to operate the new machinery we were acquiring. But it was precisely this insistence on equality not only of earnings but also of workload which frustrated our every attempt to work out an acceptable compromise.

A special subcommittee of the Southampton Modernisation Committee was formed. On many occasions it was chaired by Ernie Allen. After intensive work we formulated a scheme based on 'team rotation' which we believed to represent the best chance of effecting a workable compromise. It depended, however, on the introduction to our berths of a four-shift system, as opposed to the three shifts which were worked at the BTDB's, and required four fixed teams of men operating on consecutive weeks followed by a period when they worked in other areas of the port. It was hoped that, functioning over a period of several months, this solution might provide the essential equality factor.

I realised as I put forward some of these suggestions that they would undoubtedly present substantial problems for the BTDB, who would inevitably face pressure to introduce similar arrangements – changes the BTDB did not require and could not afford – for their own berths.

The unions were not slow to exploit this situation. At one meeting a burly yet normally reticent shop steward, sitting next to me, spoke in favour of the four-team solution in a way I would not have dared to. As he sat down, having received a mixed reception, he pulled out an empty cigarette packet and scrawled on it: 'I done it for you, guv!' Subsequently the four-team solution, in my view the only one that might have provided a hope of efficiency except for that of direct employment, was put to the vote. The issue which TGWU dockers had to decide was whether to accept the four-shift system for 204/5 berths, while retaining a three-shift system for 201/2, and ordinary daywork hours plus overtime on the conventional berths. This would have effectively separated berths 204/5 from the rest of the port. Ernie considered the position so important that, for the first time at Southampton, a secret ballot was held.

Once again the issue of equality proved all-important. Union Castle still used half of the men daily, and their interests as well as those of the BTDB lay without doubt in maintaining the status quo.

When the votes were counted it was found that the four-shift system had been narrowly defeated. The port authority, as one Sunday newspaper was quick to speculate, must have sighed with relief, and Southampton missed its second golden opportunity to break with the past and to become the country's premier container port instead of the premier passenger port it had once been.

Time was now running out. The summer of 1971 was nearly over and the first Japanese ship was due in February 1972. Our licence application still lay on the table, and we were no nearer a satisfactory solution to the employment problem. To add to the uncertainties over efficiency, it now became clear that the decision not to insist on employing our own labour was likely to be expensive. Although it was true that SCS would not have the financial responsibility consequent upon direct employment of personnel, we soon found out that the BTDB, and the Southampton Cargo Handling Company in particular, were determined to levy a very substantial surcharge on the men's wages (in the case of the Southampton Cargo Handling Company over 100 per cent) for the use of their services. There was, of course, an entitlement to a reasonable payment for overheads, but we could hardly be blamed if we sometimes felt that we were subsidising not only the remainder of the port of Southampton but possibly some of the BTDB's other 18 ports as well! These two major concerns – the way in which labour was deployed and the cost which flowed from it – were to remain with us for many years.

Meanwhile SCS had built up a management team second to none and had devised operational systems, based largely on OCL/ACT experience, that were to become the envy of terminals worldwide. When troubles hit us later, our German and Japanese counterparts frequently commiserated with us: 'There's nothing wrong with your heads, it's your hands and feet that are the problem!'

If we were to be ready by February 1972 we needed some labour right now. Training had to be done and the terms of employment had to be decided. The BTDB, who had much at stake in seeing the new terminal launched peaceably, were naturally anxious: no sensible talks could now take place with the various trade unions as to how they were to work for us under their present employers until the threat, as they saw it, of the licence application had been withdrawn.

The British shipowners, committed to providing a terminal for their foreign partners by February 1972, had the recent memory of the Tilbury ban to haunt them. My board was reluctant to withdraw the licence application, and when it finally did so reserved the right to reinstate it should it be dissatisfied with either the level of efficiency or the costs of labour. That licence application was to hang like the sword of Damocles over our heads for several years to come.

Withdrawal of the licence application opened the way for us to secure labour in all the various grades, some because we needed them and others because precedent, particularly at berths 201/2, dictated that we should have them. SCS staff had done a fine job in designing the operational methods, and there was a genuine desire on behalf of the unions and the men to make sure, with the eyes of the world upon them, that the service got off to a good start. But I and many of my closest colleagues continued to be extremely worried. It was now evident that we were inevitably to inherit from berths 201/2 many of what we considered to be inadequate working arrangements. A typical instance was that only two shifts per day could be provided on a 'guaranteed' basis: the third was to be dependent on 'volunteers' for overtime being available elsewhere in the port, and the number of individuals 'volunteering' depended on who was next in turn for overtime under the 'equality' arrangements. A man was permitted to work a turn of overtime only after he had completed six turns of normal working.

I remember, that Christmas, having to deliver at Dock House a letter from my board questioning whether, given our grave doubts as to how the operation would function, we ought to start the service at all. A few days later, a top-level meeting was held in London to make the decision. We lunched with Sir Andrew Crichton. After a full discussion of all sides of the question, Sir Andrew summed up by saying it was 'a time to be bold'. The decision was made to go ahead. At that stage it was probably inevitable. After all, we had no personal experience of Southampton, but the Southampton people themselves said it would work. Who were we to take a dismal view? Nevertheless, the overriding factor was undoubtedly the question of 'face'.

The British shipowners had suffered a massive setback during the Tilbury ban, when alone among their European partners they had been unable to offer terminal services as promised. They did not wish to enter that particular ball-game again, particularly as their partners were now

97

the West Germans and the Japanese. Kerry (subsequently Sir Kerry) St Johnston, later to become Chairman of OCL, was despatched at once to tell the Japanese of our decision, and I was asked to accompany him. It was only a short walk to their city office, and we sat down opposite about eight Japanese men, who awaited our decision with predictable inscrutability. Kerry launched into his preamble, explaining some of the difficulties we were facing. The inscrutability on the other side intensified. If I had been Kerry I think I would have been tempted to change my story at this stage, but he was an expert and carried on to claim that Southampton would be open on time to receive the first vessel, NYK's *Kamakura Maru*. For what seemed to me like an endless half minute or so, there was no reaction of any kind. Then at last their chairman looked to left and to right, received nods of assent, and the atmosphere changed immediately to one of congratulation and joviality. At least in their eyes, we had evidently made the right decision.

Southampton was proving to be a full-time job but at the same time I had an unenviable distraction. In the two years since Devlin Stage Two our family company in London – Hovey Antwerp Ltd – had been almost alone in increasing its speed of work and rates of daily output, due above all to good local management and to the excellent employer/employee relationship which we had fostered over the years. Unfortunately, the work itself now began to disappear, as the Scandinavian trades on which our Millwall business depended began to containerise and, in many cases, decided to abandon London for East Coast ports, notably Felixstowe. The position was finally reached in which we could not sustain the cost of our 300-odd employees. No other course was open but to be as generous as possible with severance pay, to put the company into voluntary liquidation and to return our stevedore employees – as was their right – to the Port of London Authority.

One of the saddest occasions of my life was when I had to attend, together with the full Hovey Antwerp Board, a meeting with all our employees at Millwall, to break the news of the closure to them. It was a tense occasion, as might have been expected, but there was little rancour. Only one snide comment was directed at me: 'It's alright for you, you've got a job with the Ben Line.' Even on that score, I had a message afterwards from our union official, that the overwhelming majority of our men wished to dissassociate themselves from that remark. Nevertheless it was a sad day, and although in retrospect the closure was inevitable, it marked the end of an era, the end of my family's 100 year association with Millwall Dock. We were able to keep the flag of Hovey Antwerp flying a little longer at Tilbury, as the terminal operating company for Swedish Lloyd. However, eventually, Swedish Lloyd became part of the Brostrom organisation, and the new owners decided that they wished to take over themselves the running of their Tilbury Terminal. The sale to them of the remaining Hovey Antwerp interests at Tilbury finally ended my family's association through four generations with the Port of London.

Perhaps this is the time and place to add a postscript on the Port of London subsequent to my departure. The loss of the Far East trades to Southampton and of other trades to Felixstowe resulted in a contraction of business which proved fatal to the private employing companies which had been licensed under the Devlin arrangements. In many cases they had striven to make the new systems a success, but loss of business to other ports as a result of the change to containerisation was something with which they could not cope. One by one they found that their workload could not sustain the number of their employees, and they were forced to return men to the PLA which, as residual employer, was obliged to accept them. In the end all of them, including the largest – Scruttons Maltby – were obliged to close, and with their closure came the end of an era and the loss of a wealth of expertise to London. The Port Authority, which inherited what remained of their business, had also to absorb far more men than could be justified, and the economic problems involving in reducing the burden of overmanning lay like a blight over the port for two decades, and hastened the closure of the upriver docks. Today, apart from the riverside wharves, only Tilbury remains of the port which once straddled the Thames from London Bridge to Gravesend.

2   The Far East trade

From the moment of decision until mid-February 1972, when the *Kamakura Maru* docked at Southampton, it was all systems go. In line with the port's wish to please, a degree of priority was undoubtedly given to the ship and, despite continual breakdowns with a new container crane and abysmal weather, the ship sailed to time and we duly received the plaudits of NYK. That first ship call was never to be forgotten. On the evening of her arrival nearly a foot of snow fell in Southampton, an unheard-of event and never to be repeated during my 15 years in the port. I was staying with my wife at the Post House Hotel just outside the dock gates so that I could be near to the scene of action. During the night I got out of bed twice to drive to the terminal and see how the workers were getting on. In the morning I picked up my chairman and drove in for the same purpose. On arrival I promptly ran the car off the unmarked dock road and we got bogged down in a snowdrift. A celebratory luncheon for the mayor and civic dignitaries the next day, planned to have been hosted by NYK at the Post House Hotel, had to be cancelled as the roads were virtually impassable.

The service was subject to a gradual build-up as the 17 ships being built – eight for the British, four for the West Germans and five for the Japanese – were delivered. They were the largest container ships ever to have been built, and for years to come; each was about the size of the QE2!

In the early stages we were not subject to much pressure, although there were obvious deficiencies in the labour arrangements. The third shift was often not available. On the other two shifts individuals were coming and going on an almost daily basis. Our dedicated shift managers rarely knew who was working for them and had no chance whatsoever to build up a meaningful relationship. The situation was probably saved in those early days through the dedication of the SCS staff. I had recruited the managers who were in the main ex-seafarers, from a wealth of talent displaced by the numbers of conventional vessels being withdrawn from service. They, and indeed all our SCS personnel, were wholly dedicated to the success of the operation, and were able, by dint of sheer hard work and often long hours, to remedy to some extent the deficiencies of the labour supplied by the BTDB. Fortunately I had won one major victory in discussion with the TGWU. On the grounds of safety I had been able to escape from the precedents set at berths 201/2 whereby each straddle carrier had to be accompanied by a checker on the ground who passed the driver instructions as to which container he was to handle next. Fortunately there had as yet been no fatalities at berths 201/2 as a result of this system, which reminded me of the men with red flags who preceded the earliest road locomotives (at least one fatality followed later). At SCS we devised a system of radio control from a central point, whereby a controller, sitting in an office rather like an airport control tower, could communicate directly with a number of straddle carriers, thus avoiding the necessity to have anybody on the ground. This flouted all the chain-of-command arguments about dockers taking instruction from foremen, etc., but the safety factor was so strong that we won the day. It was probably this system which enabled us to survive the early years of operation. Also at a very early stage we began to consider the use of computer techniques to improve our control systems, not so much because they were strictly necessary but because they enabled us to compensate for some of the deficiencies caused by the way labour was provided.

It was very much a question of taking one day at a time, and dealing with the many problems as they arose. SCS was determined to succeed in spite of the labour difficulties, spurred on not only by professional pride but also by a determination to dumbfound those in Southampton – and there were many – who considered it merely a question of time before SCS collapsed.

It should be made quite clear that the principal fault lay not with the ordinary dockworkers – or, indeed, any other workers at Southampton – but with the organisation of labour in the port. This was, from our point of view, sadly deficient, providing as it did no form of reliability or the job-identification so essential in the kind of specialised and sophisticated operations we were being asked to perform. The men at Southampton subsequently faced very substantial criticism, but it should be stated plainly that they were, in my experience, no better and no worse than those in any other British port.

Because lack of money was no obstacle to us, we were in the early years constantly trying to improve performance by buying more machinery and engaging more straddle drivers. Above all, we strove to provide three stable shifts, over seven days, on which we could always rely. Time and again we ran up against the major obstacle of 'equality'. The unions insisted that, if we had these facilities, then berths 201/2 must have them as well. But BTDB did not want them, their customers being content with the service they were receiving and unwilling to pay for the better service we could provide. For Union Castle, the prime user of the port, the main concern was to despatch their liners to time every Thursday. Shift systems were a supreme irrelevance to them; the pressures which we had to exert could act only to their detriment. In despair, my board from time to time played the card of the licence application, threatening to resubmit it in view of the failure of the existing system to provide us with the service we needed. These episodes always ended in bad blood, endangering not only the smooth running of the port but also the finances of the BTDB; they invariably involved abrupt and sometimes unhelpful chairman-to-chairman conversations between Sir Humphrey Browne of the BTDB and Ronald (subsequently Sir Ronald) Swayne who had by now succeeded Sir Andrew Crichton as chairman of OCL.

It was at about this time that my chairman and I, in an effort to find a way through an impasse which was generating so much acrimony, devised an alternative to direct employment by SCS in such a way that it might achieve the necessary efficiency. The principle we hit upon came to be known as that of the 'discrete labour force'. It involved the provision of a number of BTDB employees to work solely for SCS. This, in course of time, became the joint policy of the BTDB and SCS. Once again, however, it fell foul of the unions' principle of 'equality'.

By the latter part of 1973 all the ships had been delivered and the service was in full swing. It swiftly became apparent that Southampton was way below the other European ports (indeed all ports in the service, with the exception of Port Kelang in Malaysia) in terms of efficiency. Unless the situation could be rectified, there was a real fear that the Trio Lines consortium might pull out of Southampton.

An added complication was the impact of government financial policy. In the aftermath of the oil crisis of the early 1970s, both Labour and

Conservative governments had resorted to policies of wage freeze or wage restraint. These went much against the grain, particularly with the TGWU, an arch proponent of free collective bargaining. The policies not only made it impossible for the employers to pay more for better service – even if we could have persuaded them to do so – but almost always created friction during the annual negotiations over wages. All this was depressing and had an adverse effect on efficiency – and, of course, was wholly against the interests of SCS.

Ronald Swayne, as OCL's Chairman, intervened personally in the situation. Sir Andrew Crichton had always stressed the overriding importance of the labour factor in any question concerning ports, and had indeed given an instruction at an early stage that I, and I alone, was to undertake personally any interface with the trade unions. Sir Andrew had had long experience in dealing with them and was a favourite with the officials and stewards, with whom he invariably hit it off in a bluff, straightforward way. The Southampton men, and no doubt those in many other ports, had a soft spot for him as well they might have done, because he had been a mighty influence towards the improvements in their working conditions encapsulated in the Devlin Report.

Swayne was no less convinced of the importance of labour but he had a rather different approach. Patrician in character and intellect, he was utterly dependable; although he perhaps did not have the inspirational charisma of Sir Andrew, he was an ideal consolidator, and a man who constantly earned one's respect. We were bedevilled by inadequacies in the labour system and increasingly worried about the cost of that labour. Swayne asked me to arrange private meetings with the TGWU. I told him forcefully that there was no complaint about the men themselves – *when they were at work*. The speed of their work anyway was largely governed by the speed of the machines they used, and the inventiveness of the SCS staff in designing swift and effective communications systems had helped to improve matters yet further.

The problem was twofold. First, as the amount of container work increased and that of conventional work decreased, with Union Castle slowly reducing its services, the union dictum that a man could work only one shift on container berths for every six shifts on conventional berths was becoming ridiculous, with the 'voluntary' evening shift from 4 to 11pm being a very hit-or-miss affair.

Second, the timekeeping in the port generally left much to be desired. This was an inheritance from the past. One of my earliest memories of Union Castle's berths at Southampton was of the near impossibility of entering the Western Docks at 11.30am or after because of the surge of men – in cars, on bicycles or on foot – hurrying to leave the docks in readiness for the lunch break that theoretically lasted from 12 noon until 1 pm.

At the container berths this situation was compounded even further by the fact that, after receiving their allocation from control, situated at the other end of the docks, the straddle-carrier drivers had, in order to satisfy the principle of equality of workload, to participate in a 'draw' to decide who should work on that particular day and who should go home. We could not afford not to have these specialist drivers when we required them and, as our workload fluctuated from day to day, we more often than not had more drivers available on our two 'regular' shifts than we needed.

Some words of explanation. When containerisation had begun at Southampton, the BTDB had tried to insist that a straddle-carrier driver, when not working, should do some other work, but by the time we commenced operations this was no longer permitted and, on the principle that idle hands make for trouble, it had gradually become accepted that surplus drivers should be sent home. The problem over fairness arose because the union insisted that every driver should have an equal amount of time at home. The felony was compounded by the fact that two men were allocated to every straddle carrier on every shift, on the grounds that one man could not be expected to drive a machine for eight hours without relief. Human nature being what it is, this meant inevitably that there was one man at work while his opposite number dallied at home. This particular Southampton characteristic – I later dubbed it the 'two-to-one syndrome' – led to the near collapse of the port in 1984.

Ronald Swayne motored over from his Wiltshire home one summer morning and we met at Romsey, from where we drove together to meet the TGWU representatives at Ernie Allen's headquarters at Transport House. He had a large conference room with a dais at one end, and presided with his usual mixture of urbanity and authority. Ronald and I looked out over a room packed with shop stewards – I believe about

30-40. It was a strange scene. Coming in from the bright summer sunshine, we could scarcely see the back of the room for cigarette smoke.

The meeting was extremely orderly. Ronald and I listed those things about which we were not satisfied, and he explained the difficulties he had had in explaining Southampton's deficiencies to his German and Japanese colleagues. Southampton had been the choice of the British lines, and he called upon the people of the port to justify the confidence they had placed in it. He explained that the situation was made more difficult for the British shipowners because Felixstowe, now emerging as a potential rival to Southampton, was proceeding from strength to strength and had become the home port of several of Trio Lines' competitors. Felixstowe was also being used for some vessels by the West German partner in Trio Lines, Hapag Lloyd, who could thus make a direct comparison between Felixstowe and Southampton, very much to the latters' detriment.

The stewards reacted responsibly, undertaking to examine all the problems in detail, but were adamant that the principle of 'equality' was sacrosanct, and they hinted darkly from time to time about the iniquity of the licence application and the disasters which would follow should it ever be resurrected. At the back of their minds I am sure they knew that, for the time being at least, the ships had nowhere else to go. Felixstowe had as yet insufficient depth of water to handle the vessels, and no other port could match Southampton's geographic advantages.

Ronald assured the stewards that we did not wish to employ our own men if only they could satisfy our requirements for efficiency, but I think everyone knew that the stewards held most of the cards. The container ships were captive customers. Southampton was still primarily a conventional port and, although they would do their best to help us, it would never be at the expense of any of the stewards' cherished dogma.

Ronald returned to London. I later heard that the shop stewards had been favourably impressed, describing him as 'a fine gentleman who looked as if he had come straight off his yacht'. They were right in the first assumption but wrong in the second. Although we received help from the stewards in trying to improve the mens' performance, little changed, as it was not the men who were at fault but the industrial politics which lay behind the working arrangements.

105

I had several eminent visitors during the early days of the terminal. One of the first was Lord Beeching, past Chairman of British Rail and a national figure as he had the formidable task of closing down the major portion of Britain's railway lines. Now he had become chairman of Furness Withy, one of the original partners of OCL. I was informed that Lord Beeching wished to visit the terminal. In view of his past associations, I decided that he ought to be interested in the activities of Freightliners, the company responsible for carrying the containers by rail from Southampton. I asked the company's manager to lay on a VIP tour of the Freightliners terminal for him, and accompanied him on it. The Freightliner management made a very thorough presentation, for which they were properly thanked, but I was a little surprised when Beeching, who seemed to be a man of few words, merely remarked to me on the way back to our own terminal: 'Why is it there?' This was a reference to the fact that the railway lines at Southampton do not run alongside the quay, where the cranes could have lifted containers straight from railway wagons (as is the case in some other ports). There was and is a perfectly good answer: having the railway half a mile away enables you to iron out the conflicts between a freight rail service that operates mainly at night (passenger trains tend to monopolise the daytime hours) and ships which, dependent on wind and weather, come sometimes three at a time and at other times not at all. I have to confess that on this occasion I chickened out. I told him the truth, that the decision had been made before my appointment.

During the course of the meeting Lord Beeching, a large and heavy man, sat on a settee in my office. I was in the middle of my usual explanation of the Southampton terminal operations, which I had never thought to be impossibly boring, when he appeared to drop off to sleep. He had very heavy eyelids, which had dropped, it seemed, resolutely and for some considerable time. Fortunately for my reputation, I did not stop speaking. He was in fact listening intently.

One of the first VIPs to visit the completed terminal was Lord Inchcape, who had just taken over as chairman of P&O – at that time OCL's second biggest shareholder. Lord Inchcape was accompanied by Ronald Swayne, the OCL Chairman, who asked me to explain to Lord Inchcape the part that SCS had played in the Southampton operations. After the briefing, we all went out to the terminal to view operations in progress. I was more than a little disconcerted when a straddle carrier lumbered towards us and Lord Inchcape, who had been asking a series of probing questions about the economics of the business, suddenly said: 'What on earth is that?' It was evidently his first experience of container terminals, at any rate straddle-carrier terminals, and I had to start from square one in my explanation. This was a healthy discipline for me, but I suspect slightly more than His Lordship had bargained for.

Much was forgiven us in the early years, particularly in view of the industrial history of the British ports, but as time passed the Germans and the Japanese, in particular, became increasingly critical of Southampton's performance. Our port was now well and truly at the bottom of the league table of the European ports, and the British lines were under constant pressure to consider a change of port at the first moment when a 'break' in the agreement with the BTDB might give them a chance to do so.

However, the first real crisis came about as a result of government policy. The oil crisis had caused inflation in Britain to rise to an inordinate degree: in one year it was at about 25 per cent. The concept of wage restraint in these circumstances caused problems throughout our industry, and nowhere more than at Southampton. SCS were demanding increased efficiency, and within reason were still prepared to pay for it. But wage-restraint policies meant that the employers in the port were not empowered to pay increases in line with the rise in the the cost of living, and consequently the workers' living standards fell. At Southampton the reaction was not withdrawal of labour – which would have meant no money at all for a workforce accustomed to high wages – but a refusal to work overtime, which brought pressure to bear on the employers but kept the men at work. On conventional ships this was not critical; Union Castle was only mildly inconvenienced. But for the container port, and for SCS in particular, overtime was crucial as, under the port-wide regulations providing for 'equality', the evening shift from 4 to 11pm was worked on a 'voluntary' basis. At a stroke, the output of 204/5 berths was cut by a third, and the container ship owners had to bear the brunt. Tempers quite naturally began to flare. The shipowners blamed the employers; the employers blamed the government; and the unions were able to say that they were only acting within their agreements, as overtime was entirely 'voluntary'.

Around now the shipowners were becoming more and more worried about the costs of Southampton. The costs of the terminal, the machinery and SCS and its staff were all known factors, and not in dispute. The trouble lay with the seemingly inordinate cost of supplying labour, over and above the wages of the men concerned. It had become increasingly evident that the only way of breaking this impasse lay in reapplying for a licence and separating the SCS operation from the rest of the port. Yet the potential for industrial disruption and mayhem this might cause was only too evident.

Several traumatic meetings were held at Southampton and London. My role was to cooperate as far as I could with the Southampton port management, because it was important that a common front should be maintained against the unions. My chairman and those above him did battle with their counterparts in the BTDB.

The entertainment of distinguished visitors continued to provide a welcome diversion from these industrial traumas, although there were occasions when the two functions refused to be separated.

One of the most bizarre concerned a visit by Lord Mountbatten. The chairman of Ellerman Lines, Dennis Martin-Jenkins, rang me one day to tell me that he proposed to bring Lord Mountbatten, together with Lady Ellerman, the principal shareholder in Ellerman Lines, to the terminal. Included in the party would be Sir Humphrey Browne, Chairman of the BTDB, the owners of the port, and other notabilities. I was quite specifically directed to get them all into my conference room and tell them exactly what SCS's role was at Southampton.

Lady Ellerman had been a house guest of Lord Mountbatten at Broadlands. The two of them drove over from Romsey one morning together with Dennis Martin-Jenkins. I greeted all the guests and got them settled in our conference room, with Lord Mountbatten and Lady Ellerman facing me. I proceeded to describe the role of the company. As I got to the bit where, in describing the task of modern management, I made it clear that a manager must rely not on coercion (an option which was no longer available) but on persuasion and above all on leadership, Lord Mountbatten became obviously interested and stopped me in my tracks: 'That is very interesting – I presume you are talking about the trade unions? Where are they?'

I was slightly nonplussed. The trade unions had been going through one of their periodic 'stand-offs' from their employers. Not only were they not present, but we were not talking to them. Lord Mountbatten persisted: 'I've seen the officers, and so far I'm very happy with what I've seen, but now I'd like to see the men. Where are they?'

Sir Humphrey nobly came to my rescue, and made it clear that the question should be directed at him, because the men were the BTDB's employees.

'Very well, Sir Humphrey. I'm asking you, where are they?'

Sir Humphrey tried to explain that to produce them would be difficult, because the two sides were incommunicado.

Lord Mountbatten was incisive.

'I've seen the officers, I now wish to see the men: please find them for me.'

Sir Humphrey must have known when he was beaten. After some fevered asides a message was despatched to ask the shop stewards if, in spite of the stand-off, they would be kind enough to meet with Lord Mountbatten and the employers later that day. The stewards were of course delighted and, after an excellent luncheon for Lord Mountbatten on Ellerman's *City of Edinburgh*, a meeting was held in the afternoon at which, as I understand it, Lord Mountbatten presided and was treated to rival analyses of the deadlock by Sir Humphrey, representing the employers, and the chairman of the shop stewards. I doubt very much whether any concrete result was achieved, but Dennis Martin-Jenkins later told me that he had never imagined that the visit would end in such a way.

The physical aspects of the Southampton operation were second to none, and the terminal was increasingly used as a showpiece by not only the British shipowners but also the Foreign Office, the Trade and Industry Department and other government offices.

One memorable visit was that of Admiral Lee, chairman of the Taiwanese port of Kaoschiung, which the Trio Lines used in the Far East. We decided that, after touring the terminal, we would take him and his party to a local New Forest restaurant, one of whose specialities was to decorate the tables with miniature flags. I asked my secretary to make the booking and to ask for Chinese and British flags. I gave the matter no further thought until we were sipping our pre-lunch drinks in the adjoining lounge. Suddenly I realised that I had omitted to stress that the Chinese flag should be a Nationalist one. Horrified at the possibility of an indignant Admiral Lee walking out on us, I excused myself and hurried into the dining-room. Fortunately the restaurant manager had done his homework, and had shown more common sense than I had.

The mid-1970s brought changes in the port, but these did not come about primarily as a result of any pressures we were able to exert. The reasons were far deeper and more fundamental than that. First and foremost, there was a subtle change in Southampton's attitude to containerisation. In the early years, although the BTDB had itself pioneered the new method, they had always accorded it a very secondary place in the scheme of things, and had trimmed its requirements so as to fit in with the conventional arrangements which dominated the port. When we arrived, with our no doubt extravagant-sounding demands for a completely different set of attitudes and working arrangements, we were regarded as brash newcomers who did not really understand the working environment of Southampton and would in due course learn the error of our ways. To this end we were very much left to get on with it as best we might, located as we were on the very fringes of the port – well out of sight of Dock House, the administrative hub of Southampton, which could therefore ignore us as it got on with its 'real' job of running passenger ships, ferries and above all Union Castle. Out of sight, out of mind. In those early years, although my relationship with the port director was a close and harmonious one and he and I spent many hours in his office discussing our mutual problems, I do not remember him ever visiting our terminal to see for himself what was happening.

Again and again, SCS was obliged to refine and improve the technique of its operations in order to offset the inadequacy of the labour supply. And then, in the mid-1970s, came the bombshell. Union Castle, whose continuing dominance of the port had enabled it to carry on much as before while ports like London and Liverpool were facing drastic cutbacks and ports like Felixstowe were falling over themselves to attract the new types of traffic, announced that its mail service to South Africa was to be run down and eventually to close. At the same time, the Conference Lines, which had dominated the South African trade for many years, announced that in due course their cargoes would be containerised.

Southampton could never be the same again. Hopes of the resurrection of the *Queen Mary* faded into insignificance, and people were forced to realise that the future lay in containerisation. SCS, whether Southampton liked it or not, was the acknowledged expert in the port, with a worldwide reputation for systems expertise. This included the increasing use of computers, which had been introduced at an earlier stage than in most other ports, primarily to counterbalance the effects of labour inefficiencies. Our links with the 'establishment' and with the city of Southampton itself, which had since the first flush of enthusiasm at our arrival been minimal, now began to flourish: the 'cuckoo in the nest' had the unaccustomed experience of being courted, and recognised as having a major contribution to make to the port.

Around this time I was asked by the Southampton shipowners to propose the civic toast at a reception which the Mayor hosted annually at the Civic Centre. I recalled that, when I was being persuaded to accept my appointment as General Manager of SCS, David Lloyd had said to me: 'If you take the job you can have a house in the New Forest [which I subsequently acquired] and a boat on the Solent and, once you have set up the operation, it will run itself!' I had to report to the Mayor that David had been somewhat over optimistic, and that my score was a rather miserable one out of three!

The BTDB, for its part, must have realised that the writing was on the wall. Keith (subsequently Sir Keith) Stuart, at that time new and untried in the ports industry, had already replaced Stanley Johnson as Managing Director of the BTDB. A number of circumstances contributed to a change of leadership in the port, and it became very clear that – although the industrial arrangements were just as inadequate and the performance was little improved – there was now a new determination to get to grips with the problems and to establish Southampton as the first-class container port which it should have become in 1972. It is a tragedy that some of the priorities of the port management in 1976 could not have been manifested in 1971. Had that been the case, the history of the port might have been very different.

I had for a long time been concerned at the amount of time SCS spent in sterile and unproductive argument with the port authority, when the two of us together could have been much better employed in trying to find ways of dealing with the port's very real need for organisational and industrial change. But first there had to be a realisation by the BTDB that SCS was here to stay – that we were not going to collapse and leave them to pick up the pieces – and a willingness on their part to change course and to accord whatever priority containerisation needed to protect the port's future.

All these things were beginning to happen but, before they did, Ronald Swayne made one more bold effort to break the deadlock. The Germans and Japanese were becoming so disenchanted with the constant bickering and loss of productive time that they were looking with more and more envious eyes towards Felixstowe. Felixstowe still lacked the depth of water required, but there were increasing indications that a deepening of the approach channel from the North Sea could be effected. Alternatively, such was the expense of Southampton's delays, it was estimated that it might cost little or no more to discharge all British cargo at European ports and then ferry it across the Channel in feeder vessels. The break clause in the agreement lay up ahead, and Ronald came to Southampton determined to make clear the gravity of the situation. The rest would be up to the Southampton management and men.

A full meeting of all the managers, union officials and shop stewards at Southampton was held, and Ronald gave them a stark message. Eliminate your delays and improve productivity satisfactorily or there would be no way that the British shipowners could continue to support the use of Southampton.

The shaft went home. Southampton's problem was not that it had no pride, but that its pride in its former traditions had led to an almost obsessional aversion to change. What had been good enough for the Queens and for Union Castle must surely be good enough for these upstart container operators. But now the people of the port began to realise, perhaps for the first time, that change was coming – indeed, had already come – and that they must come to grips with the consequences.

Ronald had no sooner returned to London than the first evidence of the new mood appeared. The dockers' shop stewards' leaders approached John Williams, who had recently been appointed port director and had come to Southampton with a brief to 'sort things out' and a reputation, earned in South Wales, for being tough enough to do so. The stewards made it quite clear that they, too, recognised the gravity of the situation, and asked John and myself to help them convince their members by sharing a platform with them at a mass meeting. This was something new to Southampton – as it would have been to most other ports.

The meeting was held in the men's canteen. John and I drove there together from his office; I am sure he shared my qualms over what might lie in store. Communications between employers and men were abysmal in the port industry as a whole, but they tended to be at their worst where all the labour was employed (usually by the port authority) as a single large unit. Management tended to work behind closed doors while the superintendents and foremen, and latterly the shop stewards, dealt directly with the men. I came from a small family business, and so my own view was rather different. In Hovey Antwerp we had always prided ourselves on being a reasonably happy 'family': although I did not employ anyone at Southampton apart from my own very loyal staff, I used to spend a lot of my time walking round the terminal and on the ships where the BTDB's employees were at work. This was not so much to influence the course of events as to let people who had no other visible boss know who I was and to tell them that I was prepared to listen to anything they wanted to say to me. I suppose that my father's dictum – 'There's no substitute for the guvnor' – was bearing fruit. The result was that I was relatively well known to many of the men whereas John, not long arrived from South Wales and an inheritor of the ivory-tower concept of management, was not.

The shop stewards took complete charge of the meeting, as was their prerogative. They accepted everything Ronald had said. Whether anyone liked it or not, times were changing. It was vital to their future jobs that Trio Lines remained in Southampton. Everything must be done to satisfy the customer, although at the same time, as they intimated over and over again, the situation of fairness between one man and another was fundamental to Southampton and must be maintained. They would take steps to ensure improvement in timekeeping, and would amend the rules concerning 'equality' to ensure that SCS had the men it needed at all times.

John Williams initially had a rough ride at the meeting. Introduced as the port director, he had to suffer the ignominy of remarks such as 'Who is he?' But John was determined and resilient, and made his points eloquently and effectively, stressing in particular the number of jobs which depended on Trio. I had an easier time of it – in fact, I was listened to in almost complete silence, a recognition of the seriousness of the situation. Questions to the platform were few, and all of them were positive. I recall one last question, a very good one, from a docker who was regarded as a fanatic because his religion did not allow him to strike. The chairman of the shop stewards afterwards apologised to me for his intervention: 'We have to let him have his say.' The apology was quite unnecessary.

This was perhaps one of the most constructive periods of my time in Southampton. The stewards were as good as their word. Timekeeping was greatly improved, and men were always available. Productivity increased by something like 25 per cent. Although Southampton remained near the bottom of the European league, the gap between it and the other 'bottom runners' was eliminated. I remember with delight having my photograph taken with the chairman of the shop stewards for the local paper; the picture appeared over a caption indicating joint dedication to success.

One of our most profitable and interesting liaisons was with the Royal Corps of Transport at Marchwood. They had headquarters on the opposite side of Southampton Water from the port and so had always shown a professional interest in it. Their officers were always on the lookout for advanced technical ideas, and were not slow to appreciate the professionalism of SCS as a dedicated container operator.

As soon as the terminal was complete and the operation in full swing, we started to exchange visits. The corps would send parties of officers and other ranks to be fully briefed on SCS operations, and in return I would take parties of SCS managers and staff to inspect the latest techniques the army had to offer. In addition, I used to be invited every summer to an evening garden party on the lawn of the stately home used as their officers' mess. These pleasant evenings always culminated in the pageantry of 'beating the retreat' beneath the stately cedars on the lawn.

During one exchange of visits with the Lieutenant Colonel in command, I had shown him with pride the large quantities of sophisticated equipment which had been lavished on our terminal, but had bemoaned my inability, because of the labour problems, to deploy it effectively. He, in his turn, had demonstrated the extraordinary keeness of his officers and men, but bewailed the parsimony of his political masters at the Ministry of Defence. We concluded that with my money and his attitudes we could go a long way together!

3   The South African trade

For nearly two years, from the latter part of 1975, we enjoyed relative tranquility and were able to keep our customers happy. Although costs remained very high, the general prosperity of trade was able to sustain them, and the economic stringencies of the 1980s had not yet taken hold. The tragedy – and this was perhaps the third time that Southampton had missed a golden opportunity – was that these important improvements in performance had been brought about without any change in the basic organisation of the port. Attitudes were being turned around, but the basic industrial problems of Southampton, the failure to separate conventional from container working and the multiplicity of trade unions, with all the consequent potential for industrial rivalry and discontent, remained untouched. Perhaps it was inevitable that a desperate situation should find an immediate if superficial remedy. The necessary radical surgery might have taken more time than was available, but nevertheless it was an opportunity missed.

John Williams and I were quick to use the improvements as a starting point for a close and practical collaboration dedicated to the aim of achieving a discrete labour force for SCS. The *quid pro quo* for this was SCS's tacit agreement to abandon once and for all any aspirations to go it alone with its own labour force. The weapon of the licence application was finally abandoned.

In concept, the discrete labour force meant that certain individual dockers, while continuing to be employed by the BTDB, would in effect be seconded permanently to SCS, remaining with us as long as required. The only subsequent changes in personnel would be on compassionate grounds. John and I both felt that, from an efficiency point of view, this would give the container shipowners what they wanted, a well trained and reliable labour force. We hoped that the men could be welded by our SCS staff into a team that would look inwards towards the success of berths 204/5 rather than outwards to the problems of their colleagues elsewhere in Southampton or the BTDB's other ports.

115

There was, however, the problem of cost, which depended on how much the BTDB was determined to exact for the provision of labour. At this time there was only one difference in emphasis between John and myself. He felt, perhaps because he had no authority to take any other view, that with patience the establishing of the discrete labour force could be achieved by negotiation with each of the trade unions concerned. I felt instinctively that the unions' opposition to the complete abandonment of 'equality' would mean that, whereas 75 per cent or so of the requirement might be negotiable, the remaining 25 per cent would require administrative action, namely the creation of a new employing unit. I was quite prepared to see this unit as a company jointly owned by SCS and BTDB. It could be awarded its own licence to employ. Thus 204/5 berths would be effectively separated from the rest of the port.

John and I persisted slowly but surely with our endeavours. Regular BTDB superintendents were attached to SCS to help Ernie Wright, the BTDB senior superintendent who had been from the outset the BTDB's liaison officer with SCS. He was for many years the only senior BTDB man with us, and it was his invidious task to somehow make sure that the BTDB's employees did what we wanted them to do. The choice of Ernie (by Dennis Noddings) had been an inspired one; I think that only he could have carried out this near-impossible task. A quiet and patient man, he had the confidence not only of SCS but of his own men. He became virtually an SCS man paid by the BTDB, and yet did not lose the BTDB's confidence despite the acrimony which persisted between the two organisations in the early days. SCS probably owed its survival in large part to Ernie, and BTDB certainly were very considerably in his debt.

We were able to negotiate also arrangements whereby groups of foremen were attached more or less permanently to SCS. Such was the dedication of these to 'equality' that they had worked themselves into a position where they rotated more frequently than the men they were meant to be supervising. Often, therefore, they knew less about the job than the men did, and it is small wonder that many were held in little respect by their men. To make matters worse, they changed so often that SCS staff had no chance to get to know them.

The new arrangements provided for, on each shift, what were effectively fixed teams of foremen who could work alongside their SCS counterparts. It was an expensive undertaking, because it involved putting BTDB employees on very advantageous five-team systems (whereby five teams of men rotated through three shifts) – systems which the SCS staff had always enjoyed – but I took the view that anything that allowed all the supervisory staff to work together in the common good must be worth-while.

A new factor came to be helpful to us as we maintained our levels of efficiency. In 1976 the Conference Lines formally announced that a container service to Southern Africa would commence in 1977, and invited tenders from all the main British ports for the provision of a terminal.

This trade was dominated by the South African shipping giant Safmarine which, although partly owned by British & Commonwealth (the parent company of Union Castle), had close connections with the South African establishment. There was thus no question of the British lines in the trade (OCL and Ellerman Harrison) dictating which port they were to use, even if they had wished to do so. The decision would be made on merit and, particularly, on considerations of cost.

Fortunately for Southampton, Felixstowe was still in no position to offer a suitable service, as the size of the vessels contemplated – similar to those of the Far East vessels – prohibited the use of the port. Liverpool, however, was very much in the lists, particularly since it had very strong links with Safmarine.

For Southampton it was especially important to capture the new business as it would partly compensate for the loss of jobs involved in the withdrawal of Union Castle's conventional mail service. At this critical period, therefore, we were able to point out to the men that any misdemeanour or failure to perform well would seriously jeopardize the port's chances of obtaining the contract.

Southampton had two other very important advantages. First, it had already a terminal organisation (SCS) which had developed the specialised expertise to handle container ships of a similar size. Second, although the terminal would have to be expanded by the creation of a third berth and the provision of two more cranes, the engineers who had built berths 204/5 had had the foresight to use the sand and gravel excavated from the river bed to provide deep-water berths and a turning circle for the ships to reclaim not only the land required for berths 204 and

117

205 but also the hinterland to the adjacent berth 206. Southampton therefore had a head start: berth 206 was already half-provided and could be completed just by piling a quay wall and adding a gravel and concrete-slab surface. Equally importantly, the cost of the original reclamation did not have to be recovered against the South African contract.

It was SCS, as terminal operator, who would (if successful) enter into the contract with the Southern African lines, just as it had done with the Far East consortium. Without the expertise and professionalism of SCS there was no way Southampton could have succeeded, and yet the company had to look to the BTDB for the provision of both labour and a terminal at an acceptable cost.

In the event the BTDB came up with a competitive quote for the terminal and, in spite of the gravest misgivings about the cost of the labour, the Conference Lines in due course chose SCS as their terminal operator and Southampton as their British port. The Union Castle mail service, which had handled approximately 40 per cent of British trade with Southern Africa, was to be withdrawn in the summer of 1977, and the container service, which was to handle over 90 per cent, was to be phased in as soon as its ships were available.

There is no question but that the acquisition of the Southern Africa trade put SCS, and therefore Southampton, well and truly on the container map. The enlarged terminal – three 1,000ft (305m) berths, five quay cranes and 62 acres (25 hectares) of land, servicing 28 of the largest container ships in the world, with first-class inland communication and computerised systems second to none – was the biggest single operating unit in Britain and, so far as these factors were concerned, compared well with most anywhere else in the world. Only the problems surrounding provision of labour and the cost of so doing gave rise to concern, and indeed it was this fundamental flaw which was, before many years had passed, to prove so grievous to both SCS and Southampton.

The difficulty was that SCS, as contractor to the shipping companies, held final responsibility for Southampton's performance, and it was SCS who in effect paid the men's wages through the BTDB. But SCS did not *control* the men. Although, on a day-to-day basis, they responded willingly enough to our instructions, they remained BTDB employees. All the industrial negotiations affecting their wages were with BTDB, who had to take into account the interests not only of SCS but also of their other employees in Southampton and elsewhere. The National Union of Railwaymen, in particular, operated under national agreements, and there was no way in which their members – or indeed those of any other union working at the SCS terminal – could be isolated from industrial problems that might arise somewhere else in the country. Control of the men, from an industrial as opposed to an operational point of view, rested firmly and inexorably with BTDB. SCS and the British shipowners found themselves in an invidious position: having full responsibility but no control, they had to pay through the nose for a service which they were all too often not able to get. Their foreign partners were at least as disenchanted: they had to accept their share of both the high costs and the inefficiencies. Their only avenue of complaint was to SCS but, as they knew, SCS in itself was blameless and could do nothing about it.

All this was a little way into the future. For the time being everything was sweetness and light. John Williams and I continued to advance slowly towards our aim of a discrete labour force.

But stormy weather lay not far ahead. The last Wilson administration was running into more and more economic difficulties, and was trying to introduce the 'Social Contract' combined with wage restraint. The employers were in a straightjacket and labour was dissatisfied – particularly so in the case of the TGWU, with its dedication to the principle of free collective bargaining. All this would culminate a while later in the 1978–9 'winter of discontent'.

The docks were, as usual, in the van of industrial trouble. Because no radical solution to the problems of 204/5 berths had been found, SCS was as vulnerable as it had always been. The BTDB's senior management, a tougher breed under Keith Stuart (who had by now become chairman), were determined to batten down the hatches and reduce costs wherever possible. Notably, they felt unable to continue with the expensive existing arrangements for paying foremen, because of the repercussion on their other staff. This was an unfortunate reverse in the progress towards greater efficiency.

SCS did its utmost to compensate. In particular, faced with a one-third increase in its business after the start of the Southern Africa trade, it set its face against a commensurate increase in its own manpower, and instead introduced an even more sophisticated and comprehensive on-

119

line computer control of the terminal operations. This became one of the most sophisticated in the world, and was perhaps the salvation of SCS in the dark days ahead. It also had the effect of being a morale-booster for our staff, as it was possible, because of the far greater tonnages we could handle using very few additional men, to pay a productivity salary award much greater than that allowable under the dictat of wage restraint. I recall myself and our staff trade-union representatives making a long pilgrimage to Rex House in Lower Regent Street to put our case to the government department concerned.

Another restraining factor on the men was removed at this time. Now that it was publicly known that SCS had been awarded the contract for the Southern Africa trade, and with the evidence of 206 berth being built before their very eyes, it could no longer be claimed that the future of their jobs rested entirely on good behaviour – although, in fairness, it has to be stressed that the dockers never reneged on their basic undertaking to provide labour in three shifts whenever required.

The new round of problems centred primarily around the non-docker employees of the BTDB. These men were, of course, equally vital to the performance of the terminal. With the withdrawal of Union Castle, the railway unions, the TSSA and NUR, both felt themselves very much under threat. Union Castle had been served by the railways for both passengers and freight. Passenger boat-trains from Waterloo had been the lifeblood of Southampton since anybody could remember, and cargoes of fruit were regularly taken to Nine Elms Goods Depot by train. Now the railway lines were being ripped up in both the Western and Eastern docks, and only a freightliner service to the container terminal, which required no manpower from the docks, was left. No wonder these men felt afraid of the future and, feeling they had little to lose, reacted accordingly. The Allied Trades engineering staff were only slightly less worried. Dozens of old-fashioned cranes in the old docks were being scrapped, as were the maintenance jobs which went with them. The talk everywhere was of redundancy. Although the terms offered to those prepared to go were always reasonable the scene was set for trouble. Everyone – especially the foremen, who had already suffered a reduction in their take-home pay – was worried about their money and their future.

The men were not slow to grasp the fact that a withdrawal of labour –

or, more frequently, a work-to-rule or go-slow – by any one group could exert maximum pressure on the employers by disrupting the container operations while at the same time enforcing payment of the remaining groups, who were 'prepared to work but unable to do so'. With a degree of coordination (or, as we often suspected, with the assistance of an *eminence grise* from above), the groups could take turns in making their protest without too much loss to any one of them. The pressures on the employers could thereby be sustained for months on end. I once had to report to my board that the terminal had not worked properly for 11 consecutive months!

During these difficult days, visits by notabilities were as usual a source of diversion, often of delight, and sometimes of pure comedy. The Russians and mainland Chinese were much in evidence. They were always accompanied by Foreign Office personnel and often by BTDB's officials. Communication was always through an interpreter provided by the visitors, usually a young woman (in marked contrast to the dignitaries). In spite of the difficulties of language, our visitors were always very much on the ball. Often from a military background, they were much impressed by the orderly precision of a well laid-out container port, with its serried ranks of ubiquitous boxes and its straddle carriers moving purposefully around in response to the radio directions of a controller in the distant operations room.

It was my habit to take VIPs to the wing of the ship's bridge so that we could look out over the terminal. It was an impressive sight. On one occasion I described with some justifiable pride to a Chinese Deputy Minister of Transport what was going on. He was not to be diverted from asking the most pertinent question of all through the interpreter, who announced in dulcet tones: 'The Minister asks how many men are employed there.' Bearing in mind that cost was increasingly becoming the make-or-break issue at the terminal, he earned full marks for perspicacity.

On another occasion, the BTDB announced that it was bringing down the current Shadow Minister (subsequently Minister) of Transport. Unfortunately, shortly before his arrival there was a short-lived industrial dispute at the terminal and work ceased. There seemed little point in spoiling the visit, which luckily coincided with a change of shift when there would have been no work in progress anyway. A German ship was in port. With as much nonchalance as possible we escorted our guest aboard and into the master's cabin, where he was regaled for half an hour with a mixture of German beer and conversation. He left the terminal happy with everything he had seen and quite oblivious of any industrial problems.

John Williams and I were totally at one in facing the problems, which we had inherited rather than made. John dedicated much of his time to endless meetings (most of which I attended) with the various groups of stewards to try to devise wage systems that would bring comparability and fairness between the various groups of workers. Evidence was accumulating in London that the period of relative calm was ending. I was on one occasion summoned by Ronald Swayne to give account of my stewardship to the entire board of OCL, which represented a major cross-section of the British shipping industry. I was uncertain of my reception, because I had a woeful tale to tell, but I tackled the thing head-on, reminding them of the circumstances surrounding our failure to obtain a licence to employ. I ended by listing our massive current problems. Ronald asked me directly but kindly whether in my view the board had given me an impossible task, and whether they would not now be wise to remove their investment to another port, accepting the consequent losses. I replied that I had always been taught that, when faced with problems

- you identify them
- you face up to them
- you never run away

I was convinced that the BTDB was now determined to get things right, that John Williams was the best man to do it, and that together we could succeed. In fact it was to take another seven years and at least two major crises before my prediction came true, but I do not regret what I said. Ronald was good enough to say that he thought that the Southampton leadership was the right one, and that OCL should continue its support. As always after any senior meeting of this kind, I left London with an overwhelming feeling of responsibility but at the same time the comforting knowledge that I had complete support for my determination to succeed.

One final piece of the jigsaw had to be fitted in. SCS had won the South African contract, and the first ships were due to arrive in mid-1977. We had a three-berth terminal, a slightly expanded management staff ready to handle the new business and a vastly improved computer set-up to enable it to do so. I was determined to secure total flexibility of berthing between the Far East and South African ships. Much to the annoyance of some of the old-timers in the BTDB, who insisted on calling berth 206 the 'South African berth', we put the first South African vessel on berth 204: a Far East container ship was the first to use berth 206.

What we lacked was BTDB labour. There followed the most prolonged and most difficult negotiation – particularly with the TGWU dockers – that I have ever known. We had secured the South African contract against fierce competition, and it was imperative that labour costs be kept as low as possible. We already had considerably more men on the terminal than we really needed, because of the practice of double-manning (see page 104). With the crane drivers, *triple*-manning was the order of the day. Such was the importance of these machines that it was quite reasonable to have a second driver always at the ready; but the function of the third man was beyond my comprehension, and the BTDB – despite my discreet and sometimes not-so-discreet queries – were likewise quite unable to give a comprehensible answer.

For the purpose of this negotiation, however, we had to accept the situation warts and all. I was determined not to worsen things. Because SCS would have to pay the bill, and because the bill would depend on the number of men employed, I was very much the key figure in the negotiations, although they had to be conducted under the auspices of BTDB, with the chair rotating between senior representatives of the employers and the unions.

Coincident with the improvement in the attitude of the dockers, there had been some changes in the trade unions' organisation. Ernie Allen had retired, to be succeeded by ex-docker John Ashman, whose policies were in many ways different. Ernie, as regional secretary, had involved himself directly in docks affairs, notably in the negotiations over Devlin Stage Two and those when I first came to Southampton. Partly as a result of Ernie's direct involvement, the office of docks officer, with responsibility for the docks alone, had lost some of its importance, and more and more of the real authority had devolved on the shop stewards.

John took a conscious decision to reverse this process. He remained aloof from the docks and concentrated on his regional responsibility. However, he made an important appointment to the post of docks officer, selecting Dennis Harryman, who had previously been one of the two senior shop stewards. There is a sense in which Dennis might be described as 'poacher turned gamekeeper', but his significance was much more than that. He knew the men inside out, and, as a likeable personality, he swiftly gained the confidence of SCS and was able to act as an effective bridge between employers and the moderate elements in the union, and to counterbalance the would-be disruptive efforts of some of his less moderate colleagues.

The negotiations lasted for several months and countless meetings. They were almost entirely about numbers. It was vital for the economics of the operation to have as few extra men as possible. Yet it was perfectly understandable that the union wanted to secure jobs for as many as possible of the 700 or so men which Union Castle had employed, day-in-day-out, for many years. The union was not slow to grasp the published statements that SCS would handle over 90 per cent of this trade, rather than the 40 per cent Union Castle had carried.

One way to conduct a negotiation of this kind is to hold a Dutch auction. The unions demand an extravagantly high number and the employers retort with a ridiculously low offer. The classic settlement lies somewhere in the middle. We calculated that, on the basis of increasing the labour force by the same percentage as the increase in the number of containers which the additional trade represented, the highest number of extra men we could reasonably employ was 140. For me to offer substantially less than that would inevitably mean that the unions' opening bid would be for some totally unrealistic number based on Union Castle's 700. Clearly any hope of compromising at 140 was negligible. I therefore decided on a direct and honest approach, offering precisely the number which the terminal could afford and making it quite clear that, if we were forced into taking more, the whole operation would be at risk, together with all the jobs which went with it.

But before we could get to grips with the main issue we had to fight and win a battle of principle. Fortunately, before the South African contract had been signed, I had secured an undertaking from the TGWU that, if the terminal was expanded, the increased labour force would work as an integrated team for the entire terminal, handling Far East and South African business as and when required. The shop stewards now claimed that, for the purposes of deciding the numbers, the men working the South African operation should be able to do so independently, which had historically been the case with Union Castle; this argument was much encouraged by those who were determined on designating berth 206 the 'South African berth'.

Any negotiation on numbers had necessarily to be halted while this matter of principle was settled. Time and again the stewards argued ferociously in favour of separation of berth 206, claiming historical precedent and denying the right of anyone to agree otherwise. And time and again I had to remind them of the TGWU's undertaking, recorded quite clearly in the official minutes and signed by the union officer. More acrimony was engendered over this issue than any other, and more than once I had to threaten to tell the South Africans that I could not fulfil the contract. In the end the stewards gave way, accepting the first defeat they had suffered at the hands of the employers for very many years.

But it was not a propitious start to the negotiations. My colleagues and I in SCS argued at meeting after meeting for numbers commensurate with the viability of the operations. We had to delay the start of the service before we at last got any kind of realistic response from the TGWU, a figure of about 200. We managed to convince ourselves that we could sustain about 160. We were not helped by the fact that the predicted levels of the South African trade tended to fall month by month as the talks progressed. At all these many meetings, as I emphasised over and over again the importance of the company's viability to the future jobs and security of its employees, I could sense the presence of that magic figure, 700, as if it were written on a blackboard behind me.

After some months of stalemate, accompanied by anger and frustration from the South Africans, we produced a formula which would enable us to increase marginally the 160 jobs on offer. We linked our figure of 160 to a specific processing of containers through the terminal as a whole, and made it clear that, for every extra job conceded, we would require our workforce to handle a certain additional number of containers from whatever source. We were hoping that, if the terminal worked well, we would be able to attract one or more of the smaller container trades, to other parts of the world, then being introduced. Our hopes were to be dashed.

The final figure of additional workers to which we had to agree, as the price for starting the South African service was 186. The additional 50 or so over and above our real requirement merely increased the existing overmanning, and led directly to the crises of later years.

Yet the odds were stacked against us. Obviously, the berth was already there, and SCS was contractually bound to accept the ships. Because of wage restraint, the industrial climate was becoming increasingly difficult. Above all, the invisible figure of 700 hovered above us like an avenging angel.

In retrospect, I have always believed we did quite well. After months of feeding cargo through European ports, the South African lines were at last able to use Southampton. Ellerman Harrison's magnificent new *City of Durban* inaugurated the service. Southampton entered what was perhaps its hour of finest opportunity. It was the accepted home of the largest ships and most prestigious container services. Had it been able to look forward from that point and give the shipowners the service they were entitled to expect, there is no doubt that other business would have been attracted and the cost could at least have been contained, and at best reduced.

But this was not to be.

4   The crisis of 1979–80

1978 saw a gradual worsening of the industrial climate nationwide as wage controls bit ever deeper; the culmination was of course the famous 'winter of discontent' in the following year. The BTDB was harried by a succession of major problems, nearly all related to pay comparability among their various groups of employees. John Williams did his best, but at times the problems looked insoluble. Whenever pay comparability was obtained within the container berths, one or other of the BTDB's grades outside the container berths (or indeed in one of their other ports) would be offended, and so *ad infinitum*. It became more and more obvious that only separation of the container berths from the rest of the port could be the answer. Exploratory talks were held on the possibility of splitting off the container berths, to be owned and operated by SCS and BTDB jointly, but they always foundered on the point of principle that the BTDB, perhaps because it was a nationalised industry, must itself employ all the labour.

Things all came to a head in May 1979 – in, as far as I was concerned, dramatic circumstances. The previous year I had discussed with my chairman if it would be right and proper for me to become master of my livery company in London. The Worshipful Company of Loriners had been founded in 1261, and to be master of it was a considerable honour. However, acceptance would necessitate at least weekly visits to London and, since the stormclouds were beginning to gather at Southampton, I was concerned as to whether I could afford the time. Pat Tobin was unequivocal in his advice: 'Most of the shipowners would give anything in the world to be Master of a Livery Company if they had the chance. If you have that chance, then take it.' I never regretted following his advice; I had no hesitation at the end of my year in office in telling Pat that I had been able to do my job more rather than less effectively because of my mastership. This was because an essential part of dealing with any crisis is to be able to stand apart from it and view it in perspective. My mastership provided a second-to-none forum, bringing me into contact as it did with knowledgeable people from every walk of life.

The highlight of my year of office was the annual banquet for the livery and their ladies and guests at the Mansion House, at which the master, by tradition, entertains the Lord Mayor and Lady Mayoress. The top table included the Lord Lieutenant of Hampshire and Lady Malmesbury, the Deputy Lieutenant for the Isle of Wight and Lady Nicholson, as well as the Swedish Chargé d'Affaires, a judge, and a bishop who was my former headmaster. Ronald Swayne had kindly undertaken to make the major speech of the evening for me. Business guests included Sir Peter Parker (Chairman of British Rail), Keith Stuart (Managing Director of BTDB), Frank Smith (Managing Director of Safmarine in Britain), my own chairman and many others.

When I left Southampton at lunchtime to prepare myself for the occasion, nothing was amiss, although the atmosphere in the port was as usual tense. I and my wife were to stay overnight in OCL's company flat in Belgravia; we had invited the bishop there to change into his episcopal regalia. He was in the process of doing so when the telephone rang. My deputy at Southampton reported that one of the grades had withdrawn their labour, no work was being done and worse still, by some mischance there appeared to be no senior BTDB officer available. Marooned in the flat, and encumbered by the bishop's presence, I advised him that the best thing he could do was to inform one of our own OCL directors in London.

On receipt of the news, this director had an inspiration. Ronald Swayne was, he knew, dining with me at the Mansion House that very evening, and who was to be in his company but Keith Stuart? If no other way existed, it seemed an appropriate method of discussing the problem. Fortunately I did not find out what had transpired until after the event, or I would have been very much discomfited. Ronald called on Frank Smith – never averse to a battle in a good cause – as his ally, and together they confronted Keith Stuart in an anteroom while I was blithely and unconcernedly receiving all my guests. As it turned out, little if anything was achieved by this encounter (of much more importance were the joint efforts which John Williams and I were making at Southampton), but it is a good illustration of the personal tensions that can arise in such circumstances.

A rather more welcome diversion occurred at about this time. Rightly or wrongly, we had come to be considered the showplace for containerisation so far as the shipowners were concerned; latterly that became the case with BTDB as well. Eminent people from London would arrive at very short notice and we would be expected to deal with them. It was a welcome change from the rather unromantic concept of shifting square boxes on and off container vessels.

One fairly typical visit, although its bizarre nature makes it loom large in memory, was that of the Zimbabwean Minister of Transport. This took place shortly after we had initiated the Southern Africa container service and not long after the birth of Zimbabwe. The reason for the visit came to light in the course of several conversations that evening. Zimbabwe is of course landlocked, and the imports and particularly exports on which the state lives must pass through other countries on the way to a port. The only choices available in theory were South Africa and Mozambique, but the latter country's ports, Maputo and Beira, had been more or less out of commission since the withdrawal of the Portuguese, and in any case were not equipped to handle a large container ship. Hence all the cargoes had long been channelled through the South African port of Durban. The new container service consisted of South African and European vessels, any of which might carry the Zimbabwean containers. It turned out that, for reasons of political sensitivity, the Zimbabweans were anxious not to have to depend on South African Railways and Durban, but instead to open up the Mozambique railway and the port of Maputo. In addition to the Minister of Transport and his principal civil servant, the party included the High Commissioner for Zimbabwe in London, other major dignitaries, and a bodyguard. They were accompanied on the train from London by those of my fellow directors who were interested in the South African trade. In view of their eminence I was asked to have them met at the station by two limousines. I had another pressing reason for extending these courtesies. We were having one of our bad times and virtually no work was going on at the terminal which the visitors wished to see. Putting them into a car at the station meant that they could observe the terminal from not too close a distance before the timetable demanded that we go elsewhere for dinner.

The results of this plan exceeded my wildest expectations. When the cars arrived at my office they turned out to be two huge Mercedes, with darkened windows; the drivers who jumped out to open the car doors were wearing dark Mafia-style glasses. The minister turned out to be

Dr Chinamano who, as 'General China', had some years before been Mugabe's right-hand man in the war of liberation as Commander-in-Chief of the Patriotic Front forces.

After a short talk from me about the terminal, we whisked round it in the cars, hoping that they would not notice the abundant evidence of inactivity. We then drove to my favourite country hotel, situated in the middle of the New Forest just outside Lyndhurst.

The evening was both strange and pleasant. We took our pre-dinner drinks in a delightful walled garden looking out over the New Forest. Any racial barriers which might have existed swiftly evaporated: only the bodyguard remained aloof, sitting on a garden wall and glowering at us. At dinner I sat beside Chinamano, who seemed a most benevolent and kindly old gentleman, and held an unusual conversation with him on the merits of the extended family as experienced in Africa (he was concerned about the negative attitude of youngsters to this traditional concept) and the mechanics of baking one's own bread. I then asked him whether he had seen the recent wedding of the Prince of Wales on Zimbabwean television. He explained that he had, although several weeks after the event; he added, with a twinkle in his eye, pointing across the table at the High Commissioner, 'You should ask him, he was there!'

It was interesting to see that, as a minister, he seemed to be on the best of terms with his principal civil servant, who was a white Rhodesian and had been closely connected with the Smith regime. I think that the civil servant felt a little explanation was due. During a break in the meal, the two of us wandered out into the garden partly to admire the view but largely so that he could explain the politics of the situation. The Zimbabweans were really on a goodwill mission to try and persuade anyone they could to finance the rehabilitation of the Mozambique rail link and Maputo. Interestingly, it was of no concern to them whatsoever, once the containers had reached Maputo, whether they were loaded into South African or European ships. What mattered was that they must not pass through South Africa.

The evening ended happily. Our new black friends departed into an equally black night, London-bound. I thought how lucky I was to have a bed waiting only a few miles away. Alas, this story does not have a happy ending. Chinamano was the second-in-command of Joshua Nkomo. No doubt his position must have become extremely difficult when Nkomo fell out of favour with his governmental colleagues. I was grieved when I later heard of his death: I shall always remember him as a delightful man.

John Williams and I had very many meetings with the unions during the summer, but to no avail. Cost was now becoming a determining factor. SCS and the BTDB had a joint determination to limit or reduce it wherever possible. For the first time in many years the unions were facing a resolute management. Costs had to be contained: in this the port's management was backed by the shipowners in what had become an increasingly competitive world.

We in SCS were in the stupid position of having to pay, week by week, huge sums of money for men supplied by the BTDB who would not work, could not work or who worked inadequately. My instructions were to continue cooperating harmoniously with the BTDB at port level and to leave the politics to London, but the pressures grew to such an extent that in the autumn I was obliged to tell a very downcast John Williams that, if his men were not prepared to work properly, I was not prepared to pay for them. Perhaps predictably, John's reply − couched more in sorrow than in anger − was that, if I was not prepared to pay, he could not let me have the labour.

At least the cards were on the table. The terminal remained closed for the best part of three months while the politics of the case were argued over in London. What was finally brought into the open was the ridiculous position whereby the British shipowners, through SCS, carried the full financial responsibility for running the terminal yet lacked control of the labour necessary for the work to be carried out. From the moment when the terminal was first closed for those three months it was clear that it could never reopen on the same basis.

My chief concern was for my own staff, numbering about 200. They were innocent bystanders, and it was to them that virtually all the credit for Southampton's success was due.

It still seemed to me that separation of the SCS terminal from the remainder of the port was the only solution. I canvassed locally the possibility of floating a new company − with shareholders from both within and without the shipping industry − to purchase the container berths from the BTDB and to take over the responsibility for running a terminal employing its own labour. I even asked John Ashman whether, in these circumstances, he would do a deal with me as a new employer. His answer was unequivocal: if his members' jobs depended on it, he would be obliged to.

However, this was not yet to be. I had snatched a week's holiday in Malta in late September, and arrived back to a scheduled SCS Board meeting in London to find there was a crisis. Henry Karsten, who had recently taken over from Pat Tobin as my chairman, was in the throes of a major argument with the BTDB. It was essential that the terminal should reopen. Most of the ships that normally docked at Southampton were using Continental ports, at considerable inconvenience and cost, whereas their competitors who customarily docked at Felixstowe were unaffected.

On the other hand, my board supported me in the principle of refusing to pay for men who would not work. After much heartsearching, a compromise was reached with the BTDB, but the shipowners were adamant that never again would they put themselves in a position of responsibility without control.

Time was of the essence. Clearly any attempt to obtain SCS control of labour would be a difficult and prolonged one. The only alternative was to insist that, if the BTDB were to have control, it must also bear direct financial responsibility to the shipowners, British and foreign alike. The contracts which SCS had formerly had with the Far East and South African consortia were therefore terminated forthwith and handed over to the BTDB. SCS still had, however, a critical part to play. It and it alone had the necessary expertise to carry out the operations, so the roles of the BTDB and SCS were reversed, with the BTDB contracting to the shipping companies and SCS acting as a subcontractor to provide the management services.

Work resumed, and SCS was temporarily saved. It was a bitter blow for the company, though, bearing in mind that its employees had behaved exemplarily whereas it was the actions of the BTDB employees that had been the cause of all the problems. I consoled my people by pointing out that their responsibility to me was the same as it had always been. However, I now had two masters: my own board in London, for the welfare of the staff, and the BTDB in Southampton, for the conduct of the operation.

It says much for the wisdom and character of John Williams that this

Aerial view of Eastern Docks, looking towards Western Docks, in the 1950s. This was the heyday of the great passenger liners. (*Associated British Ports*)

Baskets of tomatoes being discharged at
Southampton from the Channel Islands in June
1934. Hydraulic cranes are being used.
(*Associated British Ports*)

Right: Piles being driven on Berth 202, which was used temporarily by SCS prior to completion of Berths 204 and 205. (*Overseas Containers Ltd*)
Below: Piling of the main quay wall at Berths 204 and 205. The lagoon to the right will be filled in with sand and become the container stacking area. (*Overseas Containers Ltd*)

Below: View of Berths 204 and 205 shortly after completion, taken from one of the cranes on Berth 202. Two OCL vessels are on berth. (*Associated British Ports*) **Left**: The Mayor of Southampton was invited to a party to commemorate the handling of the hundred-thousandth container by Freightliners. Their gantry crane is seen loading a container onto a rail wagon. (*Derek Pratt*)

Below: Visit of the Deputy Minister of Transport of The People's Republic of China to the terminal, accompanied by the usual back-up staff and female interpreter. Such visits were a source of diversion, often of delight, and sometimes of pure comedy. (*Hythe Photographic Services Ltd*) **Right**: The end product of all our endeavours. *Benavon*, loaded to capacity, sails on her voyage to the Orient. (*Ben Line (Containers) Ltd*)

Left: HRH The Prince of Wales being received by the author, as Managing Director of Solent Container Services, in front of their Southampton office. **Below**: Bird's eye view of the Southampton Container Terminal, which today comprises three berths (1,000 metres) and 31 hectares of container stacking space. (*Associated British Ports*).

One of Southampton Container Terminals' most modern tractor units, used to pull the containers to the railhead. Their mobile equipment fleet includes 12 such machines, as well as 32 straddle carriers. (*Southampton Container Terminals*)

Aerial view of Prince Charles Container port, showing the approaches up Southampton Water, berths 201 and 202 in the middle distance and Berths 204, 205 and 206, with three ships alongside, in the foreground. (*Associated British Ports*)

new relationship was established swiftly and without rancour. He was a frequent visitor to SCS, and the new situation perhaps confirmed our dependence on one another. During this period we continued to talk privately about the possibility of a future joint company which would employ its own labour and be separate from the rest of the port. The idea received the backing of the SCS board as well as, increasingly, of John's superiors in the BTDB.

Visits to the terminal continued to provide a welcome diversion. In one case we welcomed a very major Indian shipowner, responsible for a fleet of several hundred ships. The visit was sponsored by the Department of Trade, and I was told that my visitor would be accompanied by a senior civil servant.

When they were ushered into my room, I discovered that my Indian visitor was an elderly gentleman clad in nothing more substantial than a dhoti and sandals. His escort, by contrast, was impeccably dressed in black jacket and striped trousers. The uniqueness of the occasion was heightened when my guest remarked casually that he was an early disciple of Mahatma Ghandhi and had spent a substantial part of his life incarcerated under the British Raj. Despite this rather inauspicious start, we had a pleasant meeting culminating in a visit to a Ben Line ship that happened to be in port.

I used invariably to take my visitors onto the bridge of the ship to view the terminal operations from a height of some 80ft (25m): it was a magnificent viewing platform. Unfortunately on this occasion the lift to the bridge deck was out of order, and I rather hesitatingly had to ask the shipowner whether he minded ascending about eight flights of stairs. Although he was in his eighties, he set off at a spanking pace: the civil servant and myself trailed breathlessly behind!

On another occasion the reverse happened. This time the visitor was an Egyptian admiral. Egyptian visitors always seemed to be intent on building container ports on one or other side of the Suez Canal at the Port Said entrance. I took the admiral onto another ship, and again the lift was out of order. He was overweight and looked none too fit but assured me there was no problem. Halfway up he stopped short and told me that he suffered from a heart complaint; he then insisted on carrying on up to the bridge. I could see myself becoming the centre of an international incident, and was not sorry when the visit was over.

Two factors helped John Williams and myself at this time. A Conservative government had been returned to power in 1979; although it introduced tough economic policies based on free competition, it had no time for the politics of wage restraint. This made it easier for us to deal with some of the comparability problems and helped engender better attitudes. But the second, and much more important change was inspired by the new administration's philosophy concerning privatisation. It was announced that BTDB's 19 ports were to be privatised, with the government initially retaining a 51 per cent share but eventually handing over the entire business to private enterprise. In 1983, the BTDB became Associated British Ports plc, and the change of name brought with it a refreshing change of policy in many fields. No longer was the company bound by the nationalised status of its business to confine itself to the narrow limits of port operation. Instead, it could capitalise on the value of its land and go in for property development. In every way its scope was broadened and it became, perhaps for the first time, a real commercial enterprise. Although the shipowners frequently did not agree with the new company, at least both were speaking the same language.

It was all about economics and costs. ABP undertook a major programme to cut the size of its labour force at Southampton in the interests of economy; SCS, encouraged by its principals, did the same. One of the chief beneficiaries was the idea of a joint company, free to run its own affairs – something which had long been dear to my heart.

In 1984, 13 years after our failure to acquire our own employers' licence and thus separate the SCS terminal from the remainder of the port, the seed of the idea that had germinated so often in my exploratory discussions with John Williams now came to blossom. We gained official recognition of the concept of a new operating company which, while owned 50 per cent by ABP and 50 per cent by the shipowners, would have complete financial and operating independence from either, and above all employ its own staff and labour from top to bottom. The new company would stand or fall on its own merits. John and I were convinced that it could work. But, before it could be born, we had to face what proved to be the most traumatic period of my career and one of the blackest spots in Southampton's long history.

5 The crisis of 1984—5

The period between the crises of 1979–80 and 1984–5 was, from an efficiency point of view, one of our most rewarding. But it was now, when efficiency was reaching an acceptable level, that cost became the determining factor. Southampton had been a prestige passenger port, and so the pressures on the employers to submit to blackmail had been irresistible. The resultant increases both in wages and in the numbers of men employed to do a given job had already turned it into a very high-cost port. At first this had not mattered, because the Southampton trades were some of the most lucrative in the world, but, with the passing of the passenger ships all this had changed. The mantle of the earlier profligacy fell willy-nilly on the container vessels.

In the 1970s this had not mattered much. The accent had been on efficiency, and the shipowners were by and large prepared to pay for whatever efficiency they could get. But from 1980 onward, everything was different. As they transferred their contracts from SCS to the BTDB, the shipowners made it clear that they would never again enter into long-term contracts with anyone: a year at a time was to be the standard.

Felixstowe, under an ambitious management and with a fine industrial and economic record to back it, had launched a major expansion and channel-deepening exercise, which would allow it to accept the vessels otherwise destined for Southampton. It became clear that the shipowners had at last a viable option, and that Southampton faced the dilemma of pricing itself out of business.

The comparison between Felixstowe and Southampton was interesting. Geographically, Southampton was vastly better placed in that it lay directly along the main shipping routes down the Channel. It had a distinct advantage in terms of inland communications, by both road and rail, although Felixstowe was doing its utmost to catch up. The facilities at the two ports were of much the same quality, although in respect of computer systems Southampton (because of SCS's expertise) had a head-start. But Felixstowe had a supreme advantage: it had no history as a port, whereas Southampton had had a famous history and was taking an inordinately long time to live it down. At Felixstowe the men had been recruited from the fields and their wives into the canteen. The port was developing as a family unit, with everyone having a vested interest in success. Southampton, by contrast, had inherited all the evils of greed, mismanagement and exploitation that had bedevilled the past. In Felixstowe the men looked forward to a better future for their port and themselves; at Southampton they looked backwards to the days of the passenger liners and Union Castle, and remembered not only their glories but also their iniquities. To be inspired by history and build on it is one thing: to be chained by it is very much another matter.

Southampton was a 'Scheme Port' under the Dock Labour Scheme and as such had to pay a levy of 3 per cent towards the administration of the scheme, in addition to meeting its obligations in respect of severance pay. Felixstowe had escaped inclusion in the scheme by an accident of history: at the time the scheme had been introduced, Felixstowe had employed fewer than 200 men and so did not meet the criteria for inclusion. Having to pay no levy, Felixstowe was thus assured – all other things being equal – of a competitive edge over Southampton.

When we entertained MPs we tried to keep politics out of it, but I remember being asked shortly before the election held around that time if I would receive one of the Tory ministers and the two local Tory candidates, who were presumably anxious to be 'seen'. They duly arrived, decorated with rosettes and everything else you might expect. Fortunately I was able to get them to remove these ornaments so that they were less readily distinguishable. We then bundled them into a car and took them aboard a Japanese ship, where we had the inevitable beer, safe in the knowledge that there were no votes to be won in a Japanese ship. The unfortunate pay-off was that the Tory minister lost his job on the re-election of the government: the word was that 'if you want to lose your job, go and visit SCS'!

In mid-1984 the scene was set for action. Many of the characters had however changed. John Williams had left Southampton to become MD of ABP in London, and his mantle had been assumed by Dennis Noddings, with whom I had worked happily ever since I had come to Southampton.

So far as the shipowners were concerned, Sir Ronald Swayne had been succeeded as OCL chairman by Kerry St Johnston and Alan Hatchett, the deputy chairman of OCL, had replaced Henry Karsten as chairman of SCS.

ABP, although continuing to support the long-term objective of a joint company, were determined that costs in Southampton must be reduced without delay. Keith Stuart and John Williams formed a formidable team, and in the months to come were to show a resolution I had never seen in the dock industry. The decision to cut back, in terms of both money and manpower, was theirs alone, although they were very staunchly supported by the British shipowners, who were certain that chaos and disruption would assuredly follow if the policy of retrenchment was pressed home.

In the late summer of 1984 the various unions were formally told of the reductions both in wages and in the number of men employed on the various jobs required of them. Generous retirement terms were offered to those who would be displaced, and Dennis Noddings went to endless pains to explain to the men that without these cutbacks the port was in danger of losing all its major customers.

But the men were in no mood to listen. They were led by an extremely able shop steward, Ritchie Pearce, who had in effect taken personal control of the Southampton dockers. They had good reason to respect and follow him, because he had presided over the years when the removal of wage restraint had enabled some improvement in their condition; they also no doubt gave him credit for the part he had played in the South African negotiations. Ronald Swayne once asked to meet him privately, and this was arranged at a dinner party at the White Horse, Romsey; John Ashman, Dennis Harryman and myself were also there. Ronald, who had had a distinguished army career, told me afterwards that he would have had Ritchie willingly as his sergeant at any time.

ABP's proposals fell on deaf ears, and in desperation the company named a day in October when, acceptable or not, the new rates of pay and working conditions would apply. Predictably, there was an all-out strike. The port was reduced to a standstill. Neither side was prepared to yield, and within a few days an empty and forlorn container terminal became once again the quiet abode of thousands upon thousands of seabirds.

The weeks passed. There was a massive lack of support for the Southampton men from other British ports. Some of the ships were handled at Tilbury, some at Felixstowe, some at Bristol and many at Liverpool, where the South Africans found a home. Containers were off-loaded on the Continent and came to remote ports such as Milford Haven by feeder vessel. Costs to the shipowners were high, but the country's trade continued to flow.

As Christmas approached and the stalemate reached its third month, I began to be extremely worried about the fate of my loyal servants in SCS. This time there was no sense in going it alone and talking of forming a new company. We were in it with ABP up to the hilt, and it was kill or cure. Dennis Noddings and I appeared several times on the local television station and exhorted the men to accept, pointing out, as ever, that only their acceptance could save the port and their jobs in it. The one encouraging sign was that, throughout this period, men were in very substantial numbers voluntarily accepting ABP's severance terms and leaving a port which they no doubt felt held little future for them.

My concern was also that ABP, determined to strike the hardest possible bargain, might overreach itself and win a pyrrhic victory. The shipowners, particularly the Germans and Japanese, were prepared to wait only a limited amount of time for a settlement, and the costs of diverting the cargo from Southampton were mounting daily. More and more voices suggested abandoning Southampton in favour of another port. But the British shipowners stood shoulder-to-shoulder with ABP: to abandon them at this juncture after making common cause for months past would have made little sense. But it seemed to me that everything was now a matter of timing. ABP might achieve a 100 per cent victory but find that by then their customers had deserted them: what profit would that be? On the other hand, a major victory for ABP's policies had already been won: so many men had already left the port voluntarily that the economic policy had been vindicated. Whatever their outcome, costs were bound to be substantially reduced. It seemed to me that the time was rapidly coming when settlement must be reached, even if this had to involve a degree of compromise. I was, of course, helped to this view by my fears for the SCS staff should such a settlement not be reached, but I do not think this detracted from the logic of the argument.

OCL were equally concerned about this. Keith Stuart's determination and single-mindedness were well known and admired; it may well be that he himself was moving to the same position as mine. Early in the new year I was advised by OCL that Keith would be coming to Southampton to discuss the situation, and I was invited to meet with him together with John Williams and Dennis Noddings. Asked to give my opinion, I stressed the great importance of what ABP had already achieved and my fears that the shipowners might be forced to desert Southampton for all time. As I had found on many occasions before, that when the politics were removed and individuals could come honestly together to discuss a common problem, a solution would soon be discovered. I left the others to decide whether ACAS should be asked to intervene to effect a settlement. Shortly afterwards, this plan was announced.

One other event of major importance had intervened. Ritchie Pearce, who had been largely responsible for leading his men into the impasse in which they had been without work or pay for many weeks, found himself in a blind alley. Perhaps for the first time in a generation the employers had not yielded, and showed no signs of doing so. It says much for his character that he decided that the one further service he could render the dockers who (from his viewpoint) he had served so well for so long was to quit in order to make a settlement possible.

The Bishop of Southampton, addressing the New Year's dockland service, made a prescient analysis of the situation. In issues of industrial conflict, he said, nobody is ever entirely right, innocent parties get hurt in the cross-fire, and in the last resort one or other of the main protagonists often has to retire from the scene to make agreement possible. The Bishop was a prophet in his time. An avenue, in the form of severance pay, was open to the chairman of the stewards, and the next we knew was that he had taken it and left the industry.

The knowledge came as a shock to his colleagues, who must have seen that the writing was on the wall. His successor was a much more moderate man, and had an extremely far-sighted deputy. Together they represented a far easier pair for us to deal with. It was the information about this development which perhaps enabled the group in Dock House that morning to be more content about their decision to call in ACAS.

Yet this was not to be the end of the story. ABP, holding the initiative, was determined to concede as little as possible. The newly elected senior stewards had their reputations at stake and, while realistic enough to be open to settlement, fought for the men to the very end – which was nearly the very end for the port of Southampton. The decisive talks at Winchester, presided over by ACAS, dragged on for a week with little if any progress being made. Wage levels had ceased to be the major problem, but there remained a sizeable gap between the number of men the stewards demanded on the container berths and that which the employers considered justifiable. Time was running out. The foreign shipowners were insisting on a deadline. On a Monday morning in January 1985 a meeting was held in ABP's head office in London. Keith Stuart presided, and John Williams was there to give an up-to-date progress report on the talks in Winchester, where Dennis Noddings had been constantly involved. Kerry St. Johnston and Alan Hatchett were there for OCL, and Ben Line was represented by Hamish Muirhead, such was the importance of the occasion.

Keith Stuart made his determination clear at the outset. He was as anxious as the shipowners for a settlement, but not at any price. It would make no sense for anybody if Southampton continued to operate as a loss-making port which was too expensive for the shipowners to use. The men must make further substantial concessions: if they did not, he would close the port, and dismiss the remaining men within the provisions of the Dock Labour Scheme. We managed to persuade him that in the event of concessions which, while major, did not wholly meet his demands, he would still be open to settlement. The deadline was set for the Friday of that week. If a settlement were not reached by that day, the sword of Damocles would fall.

We left ABP's head office, and I returned to Southampton with a heavy heart. It looked as if 15 years of effort to turn Southampton into a first-class container port had been wasted. Everything lay in the hands of the negotiators, particularly the shop stewards. There was nothing I or my staff could do but wait. The dockland grapevine is famous – or notorious – for the speed and accuracy of the information it disseminates, and possibly the gist of Monday's meeting percolated to Winchester. Or it may be that the joint common sense of ACAS, ABP and the stewards at the last moment prevailed. Whatever the case, on the Wednesday we heard from Winchester that the men were making major concessions and shortly afterwards that the two sides had been able to bridge the remaining gap. A settlement had at last been reached. Total disaster for Southampton, from which it would certainly not have recovered for many years, had been averted. The port was available for work forthwith.

SCS and ABP received the news with rejoicing. The British shipowners were likewise gratified, but the two consortia themselves – one dominated by foreign interests and the other substantially influenced by them – were much slower to react favourably. It was some days before a ship ventured back to the terminal, unlike the situation in 1980 when, after months of the most appalling service and the necessity of diverting their ships elsewhere, the shipowners returned with indecent haste as soon as the port was able to receive them. Their earlier rashness had probably contributed to the length of the current dispute: they were not prepared to make the same mistake twice. Trio Lines waited several weeks before resuming their full services out of Southampton, and the South African Lines took months before forsaking the temporary home they had found at Liverpool, which had given them very good service and tried very hard to retain them.

The upshot of this settlement which had cost so much by way of blood and tears were reductions of some 25 per cent in the mannings of the container berths and about 10 per cent in the men's average take-home pay. Within three months, we at SCS calculated that we had increased our productivity in terms of containers handled per hour by 25 per cent. Whether such traumas and upheavals can ever be philosophically justified is a matter of opinion, but certainly in terms of economics and efficiency the result was a triumph for good sense, and ABP, as architects of a policy for economic survival, were to be congratulated. The months ahead were to prove that the reductions in cost had no more than compensated for the excesses which had been allowed to accumulate over the years, but at least the rot had been stopped and a massive start towards regeneration had been made. Keith Stuart, on whose shoulders the major burden had fallen, must have been a particularly relieved and contented man.

The local management at Southampton, both ABP and SCS, were very aware of how near the port had come to tragedy, and of the importance the shipping companies attached to its future performance. Southampton had been given a stay of execution and must now justify it. It was also made clear by the user lines, including the Germans and Japanese, that this message must be given directly to the men themselves. I felt exactly the same. It was therefore arranged that I and Alf Pidduck, the Deputy Port Director for ABP, should address the various shift-teams, each numbering 100 or so individuals as they resumed work. The meetings were held in the dockers' rest-room in the amenity building, and involved attendance at the night, day and evening shifts. Alf spoke first, reminding the men that agreement had now been reached and that ABP depended on them to restore the reputation of the port. Alf's was the less enviable task. He was the employer, and the men had returned to work very much on the employers' terms. But Alf was an honest down-to-earth character, and set the scene admirably.

I was luckier because I represented the customers, on whom they all knew they depended. I told them bluntly that some of us had given our utmost to persuade the shipowners to give Southampton another chance. We had never lost faith in the port or those who worked in it: we had succeeded, but only by the skin of our teeth. That, in my view, gave me the right to ask for the complete cooperation and support of every individual present. I made it clear that I and my staff were dedicated to the success of the operation, but could only prevail if we had the unstinting help of everyone.

You could have heard a pin drop, and at the end the message was received with acclamation. The men had never been spoken to like this before.

Two months later I felt it right for Alf and I to hold a second set of meetings with the same men, to report back to them on the results of their endeavours and to thank them for their help. The only variation in the programme which I thought advisable was in regard to the night-shift meeting, particularly as this occurred on a Saturday night. On the first occasion some of the men had evidently, and not unreasonably, been at the pub beforehand, so that meeting was more lively than it might otherwise have been. For the repeat performance I decided that an evening meal, plus a half bottle of claret, at the Dolphin Hotel would fortify me: if you can't beat them, join them.

This series of meetings was subsequently and somewhat irreverently dubbed 'The John and Alf Act'. But, joking apart, I sincerely believe that the meetings represented something entirely new and wholly positive in the conduct of industrial communications in the docks.

We had resumed work for only a month or so when Kerry St. Johnston told me that the General Council of British Shipping, at that time led by Bill Menzies-Wilson, had invited the Prince of Wales to visit Southampton. The main purpose of the visit was to acquaint His Royal Highness with the predicament in which the British shipping industry now found itself: its fleet was diminishing and its foreign competitors were often subsidised by their governments. The prince had some years before given his name to the Southampton container port, and so it was natural that we should show it to him. He was to be taken for a visit to SCS, during which I was to explain the role of the company, to show him the conduct of operations and to introduce him to as many managers and staff as possible. I insisted on including the six or seven senior shop stewards. Next he was to be taken aboard OCL's *Cardigan Bay*, where the shipowners – who included most of the major figures in the industry – were to make their presentation on the state of British shipping. Lastly, a cocktail party was to be held aboard the ship for the prince, who had an afternoon engagement which precluded his staying for lunch.

The only problem concerned the logistics. The *Cardigan Bay* was steaming at a rate of knots from the Suez Canal, and was no doubt burning oil at a prodigious rate in order to be at its berth in time. The best she could manage was 11 am, and the royal helicopter touched down at the terminal at 10am.

By 9am the elite of the British shipping industry had gathered in my room at the terminal; one irreverent member of staff remarked that, if I locked the door and lost the key for an hour or so, some answers might be found to the industry's problems! On a more serious note, I had to tell everyone there that there was still no certainty about the time of the ship's arrival. We made three contingency plans. The first was the visit as planned. The next alternative, in the event of the ship being a little late, was that the shipowners' presentation after the tour of SCS would take place in my office, with the cocktail party being held on board the ship thereafter. The final option, in the event of the *Cardigan Bay* being very late or not showing up at all, was that the cocktail party would likewise be held in my room, on the grounds that my gin was just as good as anybody else's. Half an hour before the helicopter landed, we had still not decided which plan to go for. I was mightily relieved when Bill Menzies-Wilson finally and unequivocally decided on option two.

It was a great honour and privilege to entertain the Prince of Wales, who showed an evident interest in all that he was shown, and particularly in the people that he met. It was a fine and much appreciated reward for our staff, who had laboured so loyally through so many crises that had not been of their making. The visit was a private one, and throughout the tour the prince was entirely at ease and obviously in tune with all the staff, male and female. What pleased me most was that he was good enough to convey through his equerry after the visit that he had enjoyed himself – as I am sure he did.

I was due to retire on my 63rd birthday in September 1985, but in the event my colleagues on the SCS Board asked me to carry on till the end of the year to allow them more time to appoint a successor. The level of performance achieved from the time of resumption of work in January until I retired was such that, perhaps for the first time, I had little or no cause for concern, and was able to progress what I still consider to be my most important contribution to the future of Southampton, the separation of the port into two distinct units, each employing its own management staff and its own labour. At the outset of the 1984/85 crisis the ABP/CY Tung joint venture (which had taken over operational responsibility for berths 201/2, subsequently to become known as the Mayflower Container Terminal) had ceased to operate, and on resumption of work ABP had made it clear that it had no intention in the forseeable future of using berths 201/2 again for containers. In the next few months the berths were indeed converted to become a terminal for the import and export of motor vehicles, and the container-handling gantry cranes were removed.

The sole remaining container facility was therefore berths 204/5/6, now operated by ABP and managed for them by SCS. For the first time ABP and SCS openly agreed on a policy to set up an entirely new terminal-operating company, jointly owned on a 50:50 basis and divorced from the remainder of the port. The company would contract with any shipowners requiring its facilities, and stand or fall on its merits alone. Above all, it would employ its own people, management and labour alike. The remainder of the port would be run under the aegis of ABP, and its labour would continue to be employed by ABP.

A joint working party was established in London to investigate and if possible satisfy all relevant parties on the viability of the proposed new container company. It fell to Dennis Noddings and myself to test the water as far as the trade unions were concerned. The problems we faced were threefold:

- deciding whether we could continue to live with the multiplicity of trade unions at Southampton
- securing the separation of the two parts of the port and the acceptance of more than one employer of labour, something that none of the unions had formerly been prepared to contemplate
- ensuring that the numbers of individuals employed in the new company were such as to make it viable.

For my part, I was certain that it was essential to gain acceptance of the separation of the port and the fact that there would be a new employer. Without this – and I knew the strength of feeling on both matters – we would be nowhere. Dennis and I both felt that we could tolerate the continuation of multi-union representation, as the situation had been eased by the formation for the first time ever of a Port Negotiating Committee, representative of all the union groups, during the days of crisis. This would enable the managers of the container terminal to deal around a single table with any future problems arising from the operations. It was of course self-evident that the number of employees had to be as low as possible.

One pleasant day in June 1985, with the sun shining on the backcloth of the New Forest, Dennis and I met with John Ashman, the Regional Secretary of the TGWU, and with Dennis Harryman, his Docks Officer. It was pleasant to be able to discuss with them a project which was so clearly forward-looking and in their members' interests, and contrasted wildly with some of the hole-in-the-corner meetings I had been obliged to hold with union officials and shop stewards in an often desperate effort to conciliate between them and their employers in the dark days from which we had now thankfully emerged.

My views of the desirability of separation and of a new joint company were fairly well known to the shop stewards, with whom SCS had had a continuous dialogue even in the most difficult times, and I had had a private meeting with John Ashman at another New Forest hostelry a couple of months before to warn him of what I thought might well happen, so I am sure that John and Dennis Harryman were hardly surprised by our proposals. What probably did surprise them was that, for the first time, ABP and SCS were now proposing a new employer. To my great delight, while in no way committing themselves, neither were opposed to the idea in principle; Dennis Harryman even went out of his way to express the view that the majority of those who normally worked at the container port would support the concept. Dennis Noddings was able to assure them that the remainder of the port would be viable on its own, and would provide employment for about half the dockers. The question of numbers at the container port was the most difficult problem. Both John and Dennis Harryman appreciated the need for future viability and that this, in the last resort, depended on the numbers of men employed and the level of business at the terminal. They pointed out, however, that only a couple of months before ACAS had secured an agreement based on the employment of 75 per cent of the previous workforce in the container port: there was no way in which they would be able to persuade their men to accept separation, which they had so long and passionately resisted, and a further cut in numbers simultaneously. The price for acceptance of separation would have to be the employment of the ACAS numbers on day one. On day two, however, they would sit down with the new management of the container terminal to discuss whether projected viability required any further reduction.

Encouraged by the knowledge that our proposals were negotiable, although we expressed concern at the unions' insistence on no further reduction in numbers before separation, the working party forged ahead with its feasibility studies. In due course we produced a draft prospectus for probable shareholders. ABP and OCL, the predominating shareholder in SCS, were swift to signify agreement in principle, although they made it clear that final agreement to go ahead and form the new company would depend on the conclusion of detailed negotiations with the unions. Ben Line and Ellerman Harrison, the two minority shareholders in SCS, were much less committed, and I was asked to present the case for acceptance of the prospectus to their boards.

I flew to Edinburgh in August and addressed the Chairman of Ben Line, whom I had known ever since we were both members of the old London Shipowners' Dock Labour Committee, and several of his senior colleagues. Ben Line had suffered much from the debacles of 1980 – 1 and 1984–5 and, after ending their share in the financial responsibility for labour failures in 1981, had made it clear that they would never assume any financial responsibility for labour in a terminal again. I was now asking them to reverse that decision. I explained that, from the moment of our own failure to obtain an employers' licence in 1971, the position of the Southampton terminal had been flawed; now, for the first time, with the creation of a new independent employing company, a successful future for the container port could be predicted.

I left Edinburgh uncertain as to whether or not I had succeeded in persuading them. Subsequently I learned to my great pleasure that Ben Line Containers Ltd had agreed in principle to take a small holding in the new company. In retrospect I feel that this decision came about less because of my advocacy than through their natural reluctance to be left out of any action likely to be dominated by their larger colleague OCL.

In similar vein I met the board of Ellerman Harrison later that month. Success here would have been very sweet, because of my past family connections with Ellermans. Unfortunately it was not to be: they decided not to join, although they would continue to be associated with the enterprise through their partnership with Ben Line in Ben Line Containers Ltd. Ellermans were subsequently taken over by Trafalgar House – the end of an era, so far as I was concerned.

On 1 November 1985 I handed over control of SCS to my successor, Bob Guille. Although I continued to serve as a director until the year's end, my active participation was over.

It was with mixed feelings that I came to say my goodbyes. In 1971 I had come to a port in which containers played no more than a minor role, a port dominated by its history and bedevilled by its legacies. By a major mischance, SCS had in 1972 been sold a flawed prospectus and as a result had had to suffer more than a decade of reponsibility without control. Now in 1985, the great prize for which I had sought all these years, an independent employing company for the container port, was within my grasp, but time had run out on me.

Retirement was softened by the extreme kindness of all my colleagues. In Keith Stuart's unavoidable absence, John Williams hosted a memorable dinner in the New Forest for my wife and myself. We were similarly honoured by my shareholders – OCL, Ben Line and Ellermans

– at a truly magnificent party presided over by Alan Hatchett in the imposing surroundings of the Naval and Military Club in Piccadilly. I also valued the kindness of OCL in allowing me to host a luncheon at their London headquarters for some of my old friends and benefactors, including two chairmen of OCL, Sir Andrew Crichton and Sir Ronald Swayne, and two chairmen of SCS, Pat Tobin and Henry Karsten. It was an appropriate footnote to the many challenges and traumas which we had faced together.

Above all, however, I valued the tributes paid by all my old friends and colleagues in SCS, a company which I had been proud to create and to serve, and whose people, from top to bottom, had been intensely loyal to me. I was lucky to be able to leave on a high note. The worst was behind us: Southampton seemed about to accept the challenge which it had rejected 15 years previously, and the future appeared bright.

6   Southampton postscript

The reader will want to know how the story ends.

My colleague and former deputy, Bob Guille, took over from me as Managing Director of SCS on 1 November 1985. Bob was also, by agreement between ABP and OCL, designated prospective Managing Director of Southampton Container Terminals Ltd, the new operating company. His remit from the SCS board and the new SCT board was to open detailed negotiations with the trade unions over a working agreement for the new company, and specifically to reopen the question of the numbers of men to be accepted into the company on its formation. An increasing body of opinion on the employers' side felt that it was unacceptable, and indeed dangerous, to leave discussion on manning reductions until after the company had been formed and commenced operations. These discussions continued over many months but, although progress was made on many fronts – and, thanks to some tough negotiating, a much better working agreement than we had ever formerly managed to achieve started to emerge – the TGWU, in particular, remained unyielding on the numbers question. In addition to the union's other arguments, it reminded ABP and SCS that the ACAS agreement had been specifically for two years: in no way would the TGWU countenance reductions in the numbers then agreed before that period was up.

The starting date for the new company had been tentatively fixed as the beginning of 1987, but in the late autumn of 1986 the negotiations over the manning question were still dragging on inconclusively. ABP felt it had a commitment to introduce the new company on the date which had been promised to the men, and was also aware, no doubt, of the possibility of losing the men's support for the separation of the container port if the negotiations were unreasonably prolonged. The shipowners, however, remained quite determined to reach agreement on the ways and means of achieving subsequent reductions in manning before the new company commenced operations, and were of the view that a few months' more negotiation could well produce the desired result. (P&O may also have felt that to commit themselves to Southampton at this moment, when they were also involved with the ports of London and Felixstowe, might be to invite the attention of the Monopolies and Mergers Commission.) As the deadline approached ABP made it clear that, so far as they were concerned, Southampton Container Terminal Ltd must set up in business as from 1 January 1987. The shipowner shareholders who had intended to participate in the new company, OCL and Ben Line, promptly disassociated themselves from this date, although they made it clear that they hoped that sufficient progress on the manning issue might be made during 1987 to persuade them to become shareholders subsequently. In the meantime, ABP went ahead on its own, taking up 100 per cent of the shares, and Southampton Container Terminals started life at the beginning of 1987 as a wholly-owned ABP subsidary, with an ABP appointee, my friend Peter Doble, as general manager and employing all its own staff. SCS remained in being, owned by the shipowners, and was contracted to manage the terminal for SCT.

Thus, at the beginning of 1987, my dream of the creation of an independent operating company employing its own labour had come, after 16 years, to be a reality. Unfortunately, the management, which had hitherto been vested in SCS, now became divided, with an SCT managing director responsible for the terminal but wholly dependent on the SCS managers and staff for the day-to-day running of the operations. Fortunately the men reacted positively to the new arrangements, and accepted a degree of flexibility undreamed of a year previously. In particular, NUR cranedrivers and checkers agreed to be interchangeable, producing a substantial improvement in economy and efficiency. The dockers, for their part, agreed on a major step forward, which had always been one of my objectives: they likewise agreed to be interchangeable between all the various docker jobs on the terminal, and this again resulted in improved productivity. In order to achieve this, all the dockers had to be trained to drive straddle carriers, but thereafter all the men could be given fair treatment through rotation of dockers within the terminal rather than within the port, a concept which had been so destructive in earlier years.

Towards the end of 1986 and in the early months of 1987 major moves were also taking place within the ranks of the shipowners. P&O, as the majority shareholder in OCL, succeeded in acquiring the shareholdings of its other two partners, Ocean Transport and Trading of Liverpool and British and Commonwealth (formerly owners of Union Castle). OCL became a wholly-owned P&O subsidiary, and subsequently changed its name to P&O Containers Ltd (P&OCL). At about this time Ellerman Lines, which had been run by a management team following a buy-out from the former owners, was sold to Trafalgar House, owners of Cunard and a substantial partner in the ACT consortium. P&O also acquired the business of European Ferries, which included the Townsend Thoreson Ferry Company, and also the Felixstowe Dock and Railway Company, which owned the Port of Felixstowe. P&O were therefore now in a position of having a major interest in all the principal British container ports, Felixstowe, Tilbury and Southampton. Bob Guille was transferred to Felixstowe as Chief Executive in the spring of 1987, and James Kinniburgh succeeded him as Managing Director of SCS.

Meanwhile, the joint efforts of SCT and SCS succeeded in driving through a major training programme and capitalising on the vastly improved attitudes of the men. The customers were satisfied and the future seemed altogether more secure. A further major step was taken in the summer of 1987, when Dennis Noddings, as Port Director of Southampton, was able to negotiate the severance of a further 50 dockers from the port (at a substantial cost to ABP) and was able to ensure that the SCT mannings fell by a similar figure. This went a good deal of the way to meeting the shipowners' reservations on the manning issue, and enabled talks to be restarted with the aim of absorbing the SCS staff into SCT, thus creating a single unified management team to complete the concept of an independent terminal-operating company. The inclusion of the shipowners as part-owners of the company was an essential ingredient, not only because it showed a proper degree of commitment to Southampton but because, as long as SCT was wholly owned by ABP, it was unlikely that the men could be persuaded that SCT was indeed wholly independent and that they would accept a final division between SCT labour and ABP labour in the rest of the port.

The terms of the absorption of SCS into SCT remained to be decided, as did the proportion of the shareholding which the shipowners wished to acquire. P&O made it clear that the shipowners wished for a controlling interest of 51 per cent and Sir Keith Stuart (as he had now become), Chairman of ABP, did not demur. Ben Line likewise indicated that they wished to participate as shareholders in the new venture, although the Ellerman interests finally severed their involvement in Southampton.

The newly constituted SCT came into being on 1 July 1988. It is a truly independent terminal operating company, inheriting the tradition of excellence in management handed down by SCS and incorporating the loyalties and proud traditions of the individual port workers of Southampton. Above all, it has the opportunity to work exclusively for the success of the enterprise. It will succeed or fail on its own merit. It will not lack in friends to wish it well: as one who tried in some part to pave the way for its success, I would like to be foremost in doing so.

Summary

It was with very mixed feeling, then, that I left the world of the docks, an industry which, despite the unattractive face it frequently shows to the public, is for many of those who work in it – and certainly for me – the subject of unique interest and affection. Perhaps because it is so little known to the world at large, it has for its practitioners a special appeal, at the centre of which lies a breed of men, a wealth of tradition and even a terminology which only they can know. It is an exclusive club, with membership handed down from generation to generation, and perhaps an excess of inbreeding has caused within the family a too ready acceptance of the faults and foibles of its members.

This was the exclusive and inward-looking society, defensive because it had all too often been under attack, in which I witnessed the impact of change during my 40 years' service in the docks, and it is the story of that impact on two of our ports which I have tried to set down in this book. The events which I have described are seen very much through the eyes of individuals, and I have not tried to give a factual blow-by-blow account of the happenings of those years: a wealth of statistical detail is available in official reports on the industry. Rather, I have been concerned with people.

I undertook earlier in the book to try and draw a balance sheet of the gains and losses over my 40 years. This is no easy task, and made more difficult by the fact that there is, with hindsight, a ring of inevitability about what happened. One is therefore tempted to think that objective assessment is irrelevant.

Although I have dealt with the two ports which I know from personal experience, I suspect that, with the exception of Felixstowe and other non-traditional ports, the conclusions reached would apply to ports of similar size throughout the kingdom. Physically and operationally, both London and Southampton have been changed radically, permanently and almost beyond recognition. Only such of the men who still work in them are the same. In the Port of London, once the pride of Empire, only

Tilbury remains of all the giant dock systems which used to straddle the Thames from Tower Bridge to the sea. Today the Docklands Development Corporation is presiding over a rebirth of the areas devastated and left forlorn by the departure of the ships. An airport has been constructed on the middle road in the Royals, where once countless tons of cargo were handled from every part of the world. Today you can stand on the empty quays and watch water-skiers and wind-surfers take their pleasure. From the Docklands Light Railway on the Isle of Dogs you can get a birdseye view of the empty basins of the West India and Millwall docks, where the 'weekly boat' used to lie, surrounded on all sides by the bustle of construction and commercial activity, surely a vast improvement on the dereliction of recent years but representative of a very different social ethos and way of life from that which formerly existed there. A massive building owned by the *Daily Telegraph* now stands on the site of the Hovey-Antwerp dock office, outside which I addressed our men in 1967. The Surrey Docks have gone, as also have the Upper Docks from the Tower to Limehouse, and housing estates look down on such empty waters as remain.

Because of its geography, Southampton has not contracted physically to the same degree, but miles of its quays stand virtually unused, and in the Eastern Docks a large area has been given over to property development. Town Quay, a port since medieval times, is destined to go the same way. Were it not for the presence of industrial tenants such as Rank Hovis, Montague Meyer and Standard Telephones, it is almost certain that large areas of the Western Docks (some now granted 'Freeport' status), where the great passenger liners used to disgorge their passengers, would have followed suit.

There is little doubt that all this was made inevitable by the revolution in the economics of shipowning and of ship design, hastened perhaps by World War II and above all by the introduction of containerisation, in which I was able to play my part. The increasing size of the vessels themselves would have made contraction inevitable, particularly in the case of London, with the depth limitations imposed by the River Thames upstream of Tilbury. If the increase in dimensions of the ships was to decimate the ports, then the advent of containerisation was to do the same for the workforce.

Had it not been for the father-to-son nature of the industry the reduction in numbers might have been less traumatic. Had it not been for the achievement, after years of struggle, of a degree of security in the context of the Dock Labour Scheme and the abolition of the casual system, perhaps it would have been less resented. Whatever the circumstances, one can only deplore the social consequences: no amount of severance money could compensate for the dockers' loss of livelihood and status in society.

But there are two sides to the picture. The docklands of the pre-war years were a miserable and often squalid place. The physical work was often cruelly hard, dirty and dangerous and the men were paid as little as possible – and even that pittance only because of the protection of their unions. Amenities were primitive or non existent. Today, those who remain enjoy conditions which their fathers – and certainly their grandfathers – could not have imagined in their wildest dreams. Yesterday's manual worker, dependent on his physical strength and with only the most basic lifting gear to aid him, is today's technician, driving a machine costing perhaps £250,000. Today's dockworkers enjoy cleaner and safer conditions, virtually no hard manual labour is involved, and are paid a regular wage in accordance with their value to the enterprise in terms of productivity. They often enjoy first-class amenities while at work, including the provision of rest-rooms, showers and pleasant canteens, where they sometimes dine in the company of their managers. All of these things must be weighed in the balance against the jobs which have been lost.

And what of attitudes, and above all of productivity, on which the economic life of the nation depends? Under a casual system men had to work hard to survive, and it is no wonder that productivity was high, despite the lack of mechanical aids. But casualism – with its chronic side-effects of irresponsibility and sometimes corruption – had to go, and after World War II was, by common consent, unacceptable. In retrospect, it is a tragedy that the demise of casualism and the introduction of large-scale mechanisation were not coincidental. Had they been, the fact that the speed of the machine had become the controlling factor in productivity would have helped to offset the disastrous effect on human attitudes to work which were evident as soon as the threat of unemployment (part and parcel of the casual system) was removed. As it was, attitudes and consequently productivity declined to a catastrophic extent during the twilight period between the end of unadulterated casualism and the onset of containerisation in the 1960s.

Indeed, the legacy of casualism sadly persisted into the era of the container, and is in one form or another with us to this day: unfortunately, whether we like it or not, it has been excessively long a-dying. Positive attitudes to work and productivity can take place only within a framework of mutual responsibility, trust and, above all, a common objective between employer and employed. With the exception of those few employers who had some permanent men, such a framework simply did not exist. The institution of the National Dock Labour Board could provide only a financial safeguard, and in fact it worsened attitudes by further complicating the employer-employee relationship. The advent of decasualisation in 1967 provided the perfect opportunity to make each man feel part of his enterprise, but sadly this opportunity was missed. In part this was because of the continuance of the Dock Labour Scheme, which meant that a man's loyalty to his new employer was still suspect, but primarily it was because the employing organisations then established were too large, too impersonal, and too wedded to the past to make the necessary bold leap into the future.

Perhaps we asked too much. Adversarial attitudes had become so firmly established that only years of trauma and disappointment would be able to remove them.

I have always maintained that it is management's duty, and nobody else's, to lead. Unfortunately as I have increasingly realised, there is a time-lag before the workpeople follow. In the case of Southampton, I have identified it as about 15 years, during which leadership had to be given but little if any return was gained. Now the essential aim of such leadership within the docks must be the establishment of reasonably small self-contained units, in which the common interest of everyone, from top to bottom, in the success of the enterprise can banish the last vestiges of casualism. These units must be truly independent, standing or falling on their own merits, and nobody within them must be protected by legislation from the results of his own shortcomings.

Before I bring my story to a close it is worth emphasising, at the risk of some repetition, the evolution of the all important relationship between the shipowners and the various cargo-handling organisations in the docks, and of the critical effect of this changing relationship on the management-workforce interface and on the provision of leadership in the industry.

Prior to decasualisation the shipowners, who were rightly jealous of their reputation as employers of seafarers and office staff, with a few exceptions declined to take direct responsibility for the stevedores and dockers who worked their ships, and relied instead on a variety of stevedoring companies – some good, some bad – and on an abundance of casual labour for the profitable handling of their ships. There were many good managers and potential leaders in the stevedoring companies, but any attempt at effective long-term leadership was thwarted by the casual system and by the inescapable fact that the shipowners held the purse-strings. Some port authorities, particularly the PLA, were in a slightly better position to provide leadership, as they employed some at least of their men on a permanent basis, but they too suffered from the caprice of the shipowners who, in conventional days, could remove a ship from any particular port at will.

One of the main objectives of the Devlin Report was the establishment of proper employer-employee relationships – the *sine qua non* of successful leadership in the docks. The shipowners, only too well aware of the catastrophic record of labour relations in the 1950s and 1960s threw their full weight behind the implementation of the Devlin Report, and for the first time became massively involved in the employment of dockworkers. In London, with two major exceptions (including the port authority), every one of the surviving stevedoring companies became either wholly or partly owned by one or other of the major shipowners. The stage should have been set for a substantial improvement in employer-employee relationships and for the exercise of real forward leadership by competent managers backed by the shipowners' money and authority.

The tragedy was that the effect of containerisation – itself undoubtedly one of the reasons for the shipowners' support for the Devlin proposals – in fact drove the conventional stevedoring companies to the wall. In the private sector in London and Southampton, only those container-terminal-operating companies owned and funded by the shipowners survived and prospered. Only in these companies was the exercise of real leadership possible, but even here it was seriously compromised by a division of authority and responsibility between the shipowners, who controlled the operating companies, and the port authorities, who employed the men who worked at the container terminals.

The private stevedoring companies in the conventional trades were soon threatened by the impact of the new technology. In London many involved in short-sea trades left the port for such east-coast harbours as Felixstowe, and the loss of the massive Far East trade to Southampton was a bitter blow. Even in the Australasian trade, which remained at Tilbury, the number of men required to handle containers was far less than for the conventional ships. All this resulted in gross overmanning, because the men's jobs were protected by the National Dock Labour Scheme. Severance schemes, partly funded by the government, were instituted to alleviate the problem. One by one the private stevedoring employers found it impossible to continue on the basis of a static labour force and a declining workload. As each company ceased trading, its labour had to be distributed among those remaining in business, so making the situation even worse. Eventually all the remaining men devolved on the port authorities, who were bound to accept them, albeit reluctantly, as 'employers of last resort'.

It was disastrous for the industry that, so soon after assuming a very proper responsibility for dockworkers under the Devlin arrangements, the shipowners were driven to allow virtually the whole of their influence and authority over labour to pass to the port authorities. It was, of course, a reversion to type, and the difficulties facing them were immense, but had the shipowners been able in some way collectively to accept responsibility for the men the situation for effective management and leadership in the industry might have been very different. As it was, management of very large numbers of men devolved on port authorities which, with the possible exception of the PLA, had little experience, aptitude or organisation for the task. It became very apparent that excellence in the management of a port did not necessarily equate with the ability to manage labour relations effectively, especially in an industry in which the men worked in comparatively small isolated units. All too often management became remote and ineffectual, and leadership was conspicuous by its absence.

As we have seen, the remaining shipowner-controlled companies in the container field were to provide the catalyst for the next substantial forward advance. The increasing commercial awareness of the port authorities in the 1980s, epitomised in the privatisation of the British Transport Docks Board, opened the way to a much closer cooperation between shipowners and port authorities. This in turn made possible the evolution of the shipowner-controlled operating companies – owned jointly by the shipowners and the port authorities – employing their own management and labour at all levels. Such companies would stand or fall on their merits alone, and would give all their employees a vested interest in success. For the first time the expertise of the former stevedoring managers and the moral and financial backing of the shipowners and port authorities would be welded together to make a close employer-employee relationship and an effective forward leadership possible.

It is particularly interesting that, as this book goes to press, a development of great and potentially far-reaching importance, the setting-up of a 'dockers' co-operative', has occurred at Southampton. Because it is so clearly an extension of the philosophy outlined above, it is, I believe, worth describing in some detail.

With the absorption of SCS into SCT in July 1988 and the establishment of that company as a truly independent container terminal operation, the Port of Southampton was effectively split in two, with the conventional port being operated by ABP.

Taking advantage of the new freedom created by the abolition of the Dock Labour Scheme, ABP decided during the winter of 1989/90 to give up cargo handling in their part of the port, and to invite tenders for the work involved from private stevedoring companies. In April 1990 ABP made all its remaining cargo handling employees redundant, offering them attractive severance terms.

John Ashman, the regional secretary of the TGWU was approached by his docker members with the suggestion that a 'dockers' co-operative' be formed by the establishment of a private company in which they would be prepared to invest substantial sums of their own money. John Ashman invited Peter Doble, former executive of Dart Container and ABP, and for a time Managing Director of SCT, to form such a company.

Doble agreed, subject to the important proviso of being able to choose the number of men he required. All 189 of the portworkers made redundant by ABP were prepared to contribute £10,000 each towards the creation of the new company. Having decided that 125 was the viable number for the economic success of the operation, and after interviewing all the applicants, Doble made his choice. Included among those chosen were dockworkers, foremen, crane drivers and clerical staff, but an understanding was sought and given that all traditional demarcations would fall away and that there would be complete interchangeability between all of them. In addition, only one trade union was to be recognised, the TGWU. The men agreed that, although they would all be shareholders, management had the right to manage, and they would be subject to discipline in the normal way. Payment was to be by fixed weekly salary irrespective of work performed, only overtime being additional.

With these agreements concluded, a £100 company was purchased and renamed Southampton Cargo Handling Company, with a capital of £1 ¼ million. It subsequently became a PLC, because of the number of individual employee shareholders and the size of their per capita investment, making it a uniquely structured new venture. Appropriately, its operating headquarters is named Phoenix House. Dennis Noddings is non-executive Chairman, and Peter Doble is Managing Director. A Board of 6, all elected by mass meetings of the shareholders, includes 2 'worker directors'.

An enthusiastic response from customers has greeted the introduction of the UK's biggest stevedoring co-operative, and efficient turnarounds have been achieved on a wide variety of ships from roll on/roll off to passenger vessels.

It is because of the increasing evidence of this kind of cooperation in both the ports I have discussed that I am able to end on a high note. I believe that on balance history will record that the changes in dockland which have come about during the last 40 years were not only inevitable but to the positive advantage of those, on both sides of the industry, who are fortunate enough to remain within it.

Postscript by Keith Harper

The immediate origins of the 1989 docks strike can be traced to a brief conversation on a bright spring morning, between Whitehall and the port employers. A telephone call from the Department of Employment at 11 am on April 6, to their leader, Nick Finney was the first confirmation that the Government meant business and that plans to scrap the 42-year-old National Dock Labour Scheme were to be officially announced later that day. They had not been expecting it, although they had been pressing the Government for some years to end what had become regarded as 'a jobs for life' scheme.

The Transport and General Workers' Union, at whom the Government's action was mainly directed, was even less prepared. Its senior officials were out of town, but by that evening the union was warning, somewhat optimistically, that the country would be paralysed within weeks and its 9,400 members at 46 ports covered by the scheme, would fight to the last drop of their blood.

The fact that the dockers not only lost, but hardly drew blood, can be put down to a number of factors. The most important was the Government's timing, coupled with lucrative redundancy payments of £35,000 for dockers with more than 15 years' service. Crucially, moreover, the TGWU was frustrated by the courts from calling a national strike for almost two months, in spite of a 3-1 vote in favour in a secret ballot. By the time the employers' objections were overturned by the House of Lords, and a second ballot had apparently confirmed the dockers' willingness to back action, the moment had gone. The legal process slowed down the TGWU's plans, while thousands of dockers gratefully took the money and ran.

The speed with which the Government acted was one of political daring. Vague proposals to abolish the scheme had been lying on the desk of Norman Fowler, the Employment Secretary, since the 1987 election. But Ministers, including Mr Fowler, had always played down their real intentions. They argued that the scheme had been withering on the vine for years, and that there was no need to be deliberately provocative.

Nevertheless, the new session of Parliament the previous year had begun with a statement indicating possible action, but nothing definite. On the Tory backbenches, unanimous support existed for such a move, secured by the unrelenting campaign waged by the employers. It only needed the right moment and the Prime Minister's nod because the DE had already drafted the legislation ready to be wheeled out at the appropriate time.

Mrs Thatcher's caution was understandable. Even in times of labour docility, with the stuffing knocked out of the trade unions by four pieces of legislation during the 1980s, the Government saw little point in provoking what could have been an unnecessary, damaging national stoppage, for which the public might have held it largely responsible.

An end to the scheme, however, had always been close to Mrs Thatcher's heart. It resided uneasily in the world of Thatcherism. Since 1947 when the scheme was introduced, only registered men were allowed to perform dock work. This meant that if there was a specific job which no docker was qualified to handle, then an outsider was allowed to perform the work, so long as they were 'ghosted' by a registered employee, who merely watched the operation. Apart from the legislation, the employers saw the main obstacle to further progress in the industry as the dock labour boards, with 50 per cent union representation and an effective veto over management's 'right to manage'. Before a registered worker could be disciplined, for example, a company had to win the approval of his workmates. So few were dismissed.

When the Government made its move, several political factors combined to change its view. The first was that it required some diversion, some red meat to throw to its voracious backbenchers, who had been subjected to increasing public criticism on a whole range of issues from the health service, to poll tax and higher mortgage and interest rates.

As perceived by Ministers and finally the Prime Minister, what better way to distract attention from domestic problems than for the 'union factor' to be wheeled out once more? The calculation in Downing Street was that it was worth the risk to portray the unions again as the troublemakers, their picket lines blocking the ports, and their leaders confronting the courts.

Another more personal factor concerned the position of Mr Fowler himself. Having presided over the almost total eclipse of the DE, nothing could have helped to impress the Prime Minister more than for the Employment Secretary to have taken on what Mrs Thatcher had once described as 'one of the last bastions of institutionalised union restrictive practices'. At stake was his future advancement, and perhaps the chairmanship of the Tory Party. When Mr Fowler, dubbed by colleagues as 'the safest pair of hands in the Cabinet', failed to achieve promotion, he resigned from the Government within less than a year for family reasons.

The final important political point which the Government had to bear in mind was the impact a national docks strike could have had on the Labour Party. Apart from his position as Labour leader, Neil Kinnock also happened to be a long standing member of the TGWU. Tarring Labour with the docks dispute was certainly part of the Government's strategy. It failed because although Kinnock understandably backed the dockers, he maintained a discreet silence on whether Labour would re-introduce the scheme in the event of it being returned at the next election.

Although the employers were surprised at the April 6 announcement, they had prepared their case well in advance. In 1987, they had estimated that a docks strike was 'inevitable' and would last for six weeks. They believed correctly that the dockers would not immediately man the barricades but would heed calls from the TGWU for official action in defence of the scheme. In the months leading up to April 6, the TGWU had not been slow to test the views of its members. It led two strikes in defence of the scheme during the 1984–5 coal strike and in Christmas 1988 received the backing of a special conference of dockers' delegates for a strike on Clydeside where the employers had refused to employ registered dockers to handle cargo. It thought it knew how the membership would react.

The problem for Mr Ron Todd, the TGWU's general secretary, was whether he would be given the chance to call the dockers out while trying to operate in the strait-jacket with which the TGWU would be bound by Government legislation. The union's advisers gave clear guidance to Mr Todd that the TGWU might be subjected to severe legal and financial penalties against proceeding with a strike, even with an overwhelming majority in a ballot.

The key was the Government's untested 1982 legislation which ruled out political strikes. Mr Todd was in no doubt that if the TGWU called a strike over the scrapping of the National Dock Labour Scheme, the employers would go to court and argue that the TGWU was blatantly defying the will of Parliament. His cautionary words went unheeded by the TGWU's national docks committee. It wanted a strike ballot and it wanted it fast. Pitting himself against a unanimous decision of the 25 strong committee to launch the ballot, Mr Todd said that he wanted to approach the port employers for negotiations before pressing ahead with the vote. He admitted that open divisions existed between himself and the dockers' leaders and summoned an emergency meeting of the TGWU's general executive council to back his delaying tactics.

Mr Todd, a person who was sometimes accused of allowing his emotions to interfere with his judgement, was on this occasion tactically sound. As leader of a disparate organisation with 1.3 million members, Mr Todd knew that he could not allow a historically important but declining group of dockers, push his union into a full blooded rumpus with the courts, in which the TGWU might end up with its funds sequestrated.

On April 14, he received a mandate from the TGWU executive. The strike ballot would be delayed until after he had met with employers. If this meeting ended in failure, then the strike ballot would proceed. Afterwards, angry dockers entered the TGWU's headquarters in London, protesting at the decision. They argued that they would not allow the TGWU leader to 'break up our union', a foolish point to press under the circumstances. If they had only realised, this is just what Mr Todd was trying to protect against.

On April 18, he met the National Association of Port Employers, an organisation which was to cease to function after the Government's legislation became law. It was a lengthy affair, but the employers were only going through the motions. They knew that they had the whip hand with the Government and the law apparently lined up behind them.

Todd sensed that if the scheme was to be scrapped, the only control the union could exert would be by pressing for a national structure for port bargaining. At least, this would have given the TGWU some influence in the ports. Mr Todd's weak compromise was swiftly rejected. The employers offered little consolation, only a promise to keep national pensions arrangements for the dockers. But they warned the TGWU that they might go to court if it embarked on a strike.

Amid increasing, but by no means widespread, signs of frustration among the dockers, the TGWU launched its strike ballot, fully aware that they were heading for the courts, but powerless to do anything about it. Associated British Ports, the country's largest port employer, began the process by suing the TGWU for at least £250,000, the losses it said it had sustained through the union's decision to call the ballot.

In the middle of the legal proceedings came the ballot result, a 3-1 vote in favour of action in a 90 per cent turnout. In the vote, 6,333 voted for a strike with 2,191 against. But Mr Todd's hands were tied. In the first of the legal skirmishes, the TGWU obtained a short lived victory in the High Court. The employers were not to be put off. They decided to proceed to the High Court, forcing the TGWU to give an undertaking not to strike until it had pronounced. The employers argued that the threatened action was in response to the Government's decision to scrap the scheme, and was therefore not a lawful trade dispute.

Precious time was going to be wasted in the legal maze if the TGWU was hellbent on a strike, but there was reason enough to think that some TGWU leaders were of the opinion that they could never win a strike, even under normal circumstances. Apart from the tortuous legal process, the union was about to face a new problem. Under another piece of Government legislation, the union only had 28 days to begin its strike, otherwise the ballot lapsed and a fresh one would have to be called. Everywhere Mr Todd looked to progress the dispute, he was frustrated.

By now it was June, a full two months after the Government's industrial bombshell. It gave the industry, according to Nick Finney, NAPE's director, sufficient time to stockpile and pay off considerable numbers of dockers, whose appetite for a fight had never been tested in what, until then, was still a word war.

On June 8, the Court of Appeal granted an injunction banning the proposed strike. The judges said it would have damaged the interests of the public and the employers more than the union, but gave the TGWU leave to appeal to the Lords. Mr Todd had to wait until June 21 before the Lords threw out the Appeal Court's judgement. It sanctioned the strike, but almost three invaluable and expensive months had been lost for the TGWU.

During this time, moreover, the House of Commons had nearly finished its business. The Bill's readings were complete and the legislation scrapping the scheme was heading for Royal Assent. It gave Mr Todd just under a month to call a strike, but the employers retorted that any striking dockers would be deprived of protection and could be dismissed for breach of contract. They went on to threaten that dissident dockers might even forfeit their £35,000 severance pay.

Try though he did to keep the TGWU within the law, Mr Todd could not prevent some dockers from taking unofficial action. London and Liverpool, the traditional militant centres, were at the forefront of this splinter movement, yet never achieved their objective of a total stoppage. After a time, the unofficial action generally petered out pending the outcome of the second strike ballot.

As the dockers waited for the result, the TGWU held its biennial conference at Brighton in an atmosphere of defiance, prompted by Mr Todd's assertion that the employers were about to be involved in a dispute 'the like of which you have never seen'. Mr Todd socked it to them with rhetoric and emotion: 'Whether it is three months or six, there will be no resumption of work until every docker is reinstated and an agreement is negotiated nationally'.

In many ways, it was the high point of the dispute. In the hot house arena of a Brighton conference centre, the TGWU's campaign at least seemed to be sprouting shoots if not leaves. Mr Todd was correct to suppose that the second ballot would produce a similar result to the first. He obtained another 3-1 majority, although his troops were clearly falling by the wayside, the offer of redundancy handouts too tempting to resist.

At long last on July 12, the docks strike got underway. Most of the ports were at a standstill on that day, and the big names like London, Liverpool and Southampton, played their part. In the midst of the false euphoria, the warning signs were there. While Todd was claiming magnificent support, the employers were talking about hundreds of new applications for redundancies on top of 1,200 for the week before.

Within four days, the time for bluffing appeared to be over. The employers maintained that the return to work trickle was becoming a stream, with support for the strike close to crumbling in Grimsby and Immingham, one of the largest port operations in the country. They also threatened to sack dockers at ports where the strike was most solid.

London became the target for this operation when employers at Tilbury sacked up to 16 shop stewards and signalled that they would terminate the TGWU's bargaining rights under new contracts offered to the rest of the dockers. It was a manoeuvre which the TGWU made no attempt to head off.

When the dispute began, Mr Todd had been urged by several senior colleagues to accept the position that the old scheme could not be protected. He and the leadership were pressed to tackle the problem from the other end; that is by trying to secure a series of individual agreements with local officials which could be used by the TGWU to keep some control, however tenuous, throughout the docks.

While Mr Todd's action in defending the union in the courts, was widely commended not only inside but outside the labour movement, this refusal to build a loose framework of local deals, was thought to have counted against his intelligent generalship of a battle the TGWU could never win. The last days of the strike which finally ended on August 7, were filled with rancour and self criticism. The scheme, which had given the dockers' protection since 1947, was overtaken by Mr Fowler's legislation. Bitter confrontations developed between striking and working dockers as their leaders voted overwhelmingly to continue the strike and persuade those who had abandoned the stoppage to walk out again.

Hardening his previous cautious line, Mr Todd refused to rule out secondary picketing as part of the TGWU's efforts to breathe fresh fire into the dispute which the employers said was all but over. The action of the port employers at Tilbury had mainly contributed to Mr Todd's irrational response. As a proud Eastender, the TGWU leader objected to employers riding roughshod over the union and its members.

Throughout the country, Mr Todd watched the strike collapse. Hull and Southampton abandoned the fight. So, too, did the TGWU executive. Mr Todd travelled to Liverpool, the last pocket of resistance and made a direct plea to the dockers to recognise that continuing the strike would be futile. It coincided with the return to work of dockers at Middlesborough and Bristol, and two other main ports who continued to strike while the action was faltering.

Mr Todd faced the Liverpool dockers. Unabashed, he accepted that he had just performed a remarkable *volte face*. He told them: 'I was not going to lead dockers, who have stood solid, into oblivion. People will cry

"Judas" and "sell out" but we have a responsibility to the membership. We have got to face the realities of life. There are many battles that you lose. This was one of them.'

Liverpool was a microcosm of what occurred nationally. The dockers had been given until the day on which Todd addressed them to return to work or have their £35,000 redundancy pay removed. About 400 signed new contracts and 289 had asked for a golden handshake. From the employers' point of view, the objective had been reached. They ended up with a slimmed down labour force from 9,400 to something over 6,000 and their right to employ whom they chose. This meant no more pools of labour and new local productivity deals with enormous savings.

A carefully prepared strategy by the employers and the lure of the redundancy payments finally undid the dockers and the TGWU. In bowing to the inevitable, the union was merely repeating the past history of other industries, like coal mining and steel. It is always difficult to convince workers that jobs are worth fighting for. Money in hand, as one bitter TGWU official complained afterwards, may be only 'fool's gold', but it was too much of a temptation to resist.

Many of the dockers never returned, and those who stayed did not find their new terms and conditions as advantageous as the ones they had previously enjoyed. Until he lost his cool in the dying days of the strike, Mr Todd had played a correct game. He immediately saw the dangers to the union if it attempted to tackle the Government after its decision to abandon the national dock labour scheme.

For two years, the ports had waged a successful propaganda campaign to abandon the scheme. It was not taken seriously by Downing Street until the Prime Minister decided when her popularity started to wane that a potshot at the docks industry might pay political dividends. At the time it seemed as if it might have been a high risk strategy, but when more than 250 Tory MPs signed an early day motion calling for the legislation, to have ignored such a vocal outpouring might have caused an unnecessary internal haemorrhage. In the end, the Government was not sorry for having played safe. It meant that another traditionally powerful group of manual workers, the victims of the 1980s, followed the miners, printers, and steelworkers into the shadows, routed by a determined, opportunist combination of Government and employers.

Index